MW00656941

THE HEART *of* YOUR MOVE

The woman's relocation guide to easing the stress, comforting the soul, and listening to her heart

CAROLYN MASTERS, M.S.

The Heart of Your Move: The woman's relocation guide to easing the stress, comforting the soul, and listening to her heart

This book is written as a source of information only. The information contained in this book should by no means be considered a substitute for the advice of a qualified counselor or medical professional. The author and the publisher expressly disclaim responsibility for any adverse effects arising from the use or application of the information contained herein. Always take care and use common sense when trying out new activities.

While the author has made every effort to provide accurate information, neither the publisher nor the author assumes any responsibility for errors or for changes that occur after publication. Some links that were accessed during the manuscript research may now be inactive.

Names and identifying characteristics of the examples featured in this book have been changed for privacy purposes.

Cover design by Susan Shankin, Over and Above Creative Group.
Author photo by Merlyn Photography, Tucson, AZ.

Published by Wheatmark®
1760 East River Road, Suite 145
Tucson, Arizona 85718 USA
www.wheatmark.com

ISBN: 978-1-60494-925-4 (paperback)
ISBN: 978-1-62787-234-8 (ebook)
LCCN: 2015948308

rev201601

Dedicated to each and every woman
who makes a house a home

Contents

Foreword

The Heart of Your Move is a MUST read for any woman who is moving or anticipating a move. I have relocated so many times that I've felt like a professional mover. I kept thinking the moves would get easier each time. What I've realized is that each move still requires effort, planning, and time for adjustments.

Carolyn has amazingly described what I felt going through my moves. Clearly, having to move from one place to another is among the top stressors in life. Yes, we still have to go through the steps to move and settle in. What better way to do that than to have a transition coach right beside us.

Thanks to this book, I felt guided through the heart of my relocation journey—and you will too. It will help you reduce stress and replace it with well-deserved ease and comfort. With so many books out there about *how* to move, I had not discovered *even one* that described the emotions of moving that may be experienced throughout the entire process—until now.

I will definitely buy *The Heart of Your Move* for my friends who are moving. It's a great reminder that sanity can prevail when one is relocating.

Thanks, Carolyn, for passing on your wisdom and guiding my emotional well-being throughout my move.

—Sharon Harn, professional organizer
Sharon Harn Organizing

Acknowledgments

The expression "it takes a village" comes to mind as I reflect upon the many individuals who helped me transition my little ebook into an expanded and enhanced guide for women facing a relocation.

I am grateful to the many women who shared their personal relocation experiences and ideas. They remind us over and over again that we are not alone in mustering the courage to make major changes in our lives.

I am so thankful to our key experts who contributed stories, examples, and important insights, thus enhancing the manuscript immeasurably. A special thank you to each of you: Ariane Benefit, Sherie Broekema, Meg Files, Sharon Harn, Lauren Herring, Toni Kane, and Karen Kovacs.

Many thanks to my original manuscript editor, Barbara McNichol, who cleaned up and punched up my words through several revisions and updates. Barbara also was invaluable in assisting me with the project of interviewing key experts. She gathered so much great information that we devoted an entire chapter to our experts' ideas. Well done, my friend.

I am also indebted to Angela Smith, my extraordinary virtual assistant, for a multitude of things. I'm honored that she shared the touching story of her father's love of the land and her mother's courage after the Joplin tornado. Angela also extended lots of great ideas, reviews, and technical and personal support during the book's revision process. I'm so glad you were in my corner.

AnnaLisa Michalski is another incredible gal in my corner who offered another set of reader's eyes. Thanks for all the great suggestions and for catching those goofs—thus sparing me from great embarrassment.

To the terrific professionals at Wheatmark: Special nods to Kathryn (Kat) Gautreaux, Lori Leavitt, and Grael Norton, my favorite joyful spirits who never seemed to tire as I bombarded them with tons of publishing questions. I'm most appreciative of not only their expertise, but also their upbeat perspectives. The world's a better place with such nice people to hold our hands as we authors face the publication maze.

Words of gratitude also go to Wheatmark's Susan Wenger for giving the manuscript not one, but two thorough edits before we went to press. I so much appreciate your attention to all my questions sprinkled throughout the manuscript both times. Your patience is amazing. And to my book designer, Nicole Baron, who created the book's beautiful and relaxing page design. Thank you for hanging in there with me as we explored our ideas. I'm thrilled with you and your talents.

To Susan Shankin, my extraordinary cover designer from Over and Above Creative Group. A big thank-you hug for your willingness to bear with me and not give up on me during the creative development process. I'm delighted with your eye-appealing cover.

To Sally Rogers of Red Horse Graphics, Inc., who created the fun graphics for the book. It's a joy to experience true collaboration on our projects. As always, you are a blessing to work with.

To family and friends who encouraged me along the way:

My friend, Ann Moors, who never failed to ask me for progress reports during our regular coffee dates at Barnes and Noble.

To my sister, Mary Freeland. We became the ultimate book buddy team—sharing with each other our book projects' ups and downs during the long process of getting our books ready to publish.

And finally to my husband and sweetheart, Scott, who is perhaps delighted the most that the book is finally done. His love and patience mean so much to me.

Introduction

What matters is that one be, for a time, inwardly attentive.[1]

– Anne Morrow Lindbergh,
pioneering American aviator and author

I consider you, the reader, to be a courageous woman. How do I know that? Because you've chosen to embark on a journey of relocation. Yes, the very notion of uprooting yourself, your loved ones, and all your belongings from one spot and depositing them in another can be daunting. So if you're feeling a tad overwhelmed, welcome to the women's relocation club.

Good news! There are proven steps you can take that will bolster your bravery and give you emotional support as you make sense of your move. And they will soften the stress, too. I promise.

Specifically, in this book you'll learn insightful tips to guide you through the rough emotional terrain from start to finish. Most importantly, you'll connect with the experiences of other women. Learn through them how to tune in to your own heart's voice and find your inner wisdom. As Anne Morrow Lindbergh said, "What matters is that one be, for a time, inwardly attentive."[2]

Not only will you find ways to access that attentiveness as you do the exercises on these pages, but you can refer to a host of excellent resources, too. I've included a finely tuned selection of books and websites in the resources section so you can enrich all aspects of your journey.

Don't Be Caught in a Moving Surprise, Too

When I moved from Missouri to Arizona, I was quite surprised at just how long it took to settle in. In fact, after the boxes were unpacked and the furniture was put in place, I felt oddly UNsettled. Despite my delight with our new sunny southwest location, I experienced a sense of confusion and disconnectedness as though I were somehow out of place in this new environment. I even found myself being self-critical. *What is wrong with me?* I'd wonder and shake my head. *I've moved lots of times before! I should have my act together by now.* Heavy thoughts. And not at all energizing. I wanted to feel okay in my new environment, but I felt exactly the opposite. Why? I had to find out.

My after-the-move stress and unanticipated self-scolding motivated me to learn more about this thing called *change*. In facing this question for myself, I was determined to uncover new ways to demystify the change process millions of Americans go through every year when they move.

One especially helpful and comforting resource was William Bridges's extraordinary book *Transitions: Making Sense of Life's Changes.*[3] From Dr. Bridges's wise words and well-researched information, I created outlines and shared a mini-lesson with my husband each week. In effect, this became the precursor to my consulting work, supported by my ebook, *The Heart of Your Move*—and now this expanded book.

We found that taking the time to be *inwardly attentive* to the human side of change—plus applying the new insights to our move—helped tremendously with our own emotional relocation. The process also nudged us to communicate more frequently and discuss with each other the feelings and frustrations that surfaced during every phase of the change.

Once I finished reading Dr. Bridges's book and completed our private human-side-of-our-move program, my husband encouraged me to expand my understanding of the field of human change. Fortuitously, I discovered that Dr. Bridges offered training programs for executives and consultants. Before long, I was in San Francisco to learn firsthand from the expert himself. What a blessing I experienced connecting with him and many others who champion the emotional aspects of dealing with change—and they have much to share.[4]

As a result of my studies with Dr. Bridges and my training with leading national experts, I have spent years consulting with women in transition. The journey I've taken with them has confirmed the presence of the vital stages that naturally occur during a major change. Understanding the two dimensions of change (the art and heart of your move) will also go a long way toward *reducing your stress* and *increasing your self-confidence.*

Mapping Out Your Heart-of-Moving Journey

This guide to smoothing out the bumpy road of your relocation journey is divided into four parts:

I Become Heart Focused
II Respect Both the Art and Heart of Moving
III Discover the Three Heart-Stages
IV Explore New Resources

Part I: Become Heart Focused

The first part of this book provides you with three valuable, use-right-away tools to help you soften the stress of your move. It also includes six tips for quieting your inner moving critic—survival tips that I *had* to develop after my self-critic almost sabotaged my own move.

But you'll find more than tools and tips; they only start the process. Through a series of written exercises, you'll also open up and listen to your heart in ways that will begin to alleviate your stress. Indeed, being more open to your emotions so you can *listen attentively to what's going on inside* is the primary theme of this book.

Part II: Respect Both the Art and Heart of Moving

What is the difference between the ART of your move and the HEART of your move? In part II, you'll recognize the different patterns of behavior between the two. Why is that important? Because you'll be able to explore ways to balance both sides of the move. Each has its own critical importance; if you don't put them in balance, look out!

You'll also be coached on the value of building your own Stress Reduction Team—and how to go about doing it through the wisdom of extraordinary service providers.

Part III: Discover the Three Heart-Stages

You'll meet the three heart-stages that make up the heart and emotions of your move. You'll travel through the Gracious Goodbyes, the Muddled Middle, and the Harmonious Hellos. Each chapter in part III features definitions, in-depth information, and written exercises—all dotted with fellow movers' insights, experiences, and strategies.

You'll also be given additional opportunities to listen to your feelings and soften your stress during your relocation. Taking them to heart will make a big difference in smoothing your move, I assure you.

Part IV: Explore New Resources

After you've wrapped up the main parts of the book that feature heartfelt information and heart-focused strategies, you'll find more goodies to explore in the final part. I've highlighted some of my favorite books in this resource section. The books cover topics regarding the art and heart of moving. Parents who are moving with children will also discover resources with kid-friendly tips.

In addition to books, I've created a list of Internet resources which are grouped into two topics: general moving resources and relocation resources for seniors and caregivers.

The book then finishes up with endnotes, bibliography, index, and author bio. The last set of pages is devoted to "The Heart of Your Move" personal journal pages where you can jot down your own thoughts and ideas.

This Book as Your Guide—How It Works Best

Is it best for you to pick and choose the parts of this book that call out to you, or does it make more sense to start at the beginning of this book and read it in the order presented?

Well, the answer is "yes" and "yes." I'm a strong believer in letting you, the reader, take charge and approach its valuable content in the way that guides you best. In fact, I was adamant about including an index so you'd have another means of selecting parts that call for attention anytime during or after you experience your move.

My approach to reading a guidebook like this is to scan the front and the back first, then plunge in at page one. When I'm super busy, I combine activities such as reading while riding my exercise bicycle. Your style may be different and that's great. Remember that regardless of what I suggest, you are the boss—the CRO (chief reading officer)—of how to make this guide the most useful for you.

Heart-Focused Exercises

Because the primary goal of *The Heart of Your Move* is to encourage you to take the time to listen to your heart, I do recommend you work through every exercise.

Throughout this book, you'll be asked to record information and insights based on your own moving experiences. My clients report that interacting with the heart-focused exercises led to valuable realizations that helped them make more sense of their move. More importantly, doing the exercises helped them ease their stress. Space is provided at each writing activity, and you'll find additional room for jotting down your thoughts and reactions in a special personal journal section located at the back of the book.

Yes, I understand you're crazy busy right now, perhaps even reeling from anticipating the tasks ahead of you. Yet when you carve out precious time—*you* time—by doing these exercises, your stress levels will come down a notch or two and you'll gain respect for the emotional side of your journey.

Is This a Book or a Workbook?

The first edition of *The Heart of Your Move* was a brief ebook I created for my clients. When I decided to evolve the information into a published book, I struggled with how it should look and read. For some reason, the expanded manuscript showed signs of having a workbook-like personality. I balked at this, telling myself that women barely have time to read during a move much less do a series of writing exercises. ("You must be crazy!" my inner critic admonished me. "Relocating women have too much to do!")

Yet, like characters that come alive in a novel, the heart of my manuscript insisted on having her workbook-like voice included, too. I listened. That's why the revised book in your hands features a hands-on approach that I believe you'll appreciate.

Of course, while you're in the process of listening to your heart, you'll choose how much or how little you want to immerse yourself in writing down your answers to the questions in *The Heart of Your Move*. And don't forget the journal pages at the back of the book for those of you who'd like to jot down additional notes and insights.

Stories and Examples

You'll find that another important aspect of this book is the assortment of stories and examples from women who have undertaken relocation journeys. Their moving adventures come together into composite stories that represent a variety of experiences. Barbara

McNichol, my original manuscript editor, has also helped me interview experts connected with the relocation industry. We received so many great ideas from those conversations that we devoted a chapter to their suggestions.

Chapter Wrap-Up

My sincere hope is that you gain from this book a greater sense of patience, a more peaceful spirit, and a deeper connection with the heart of your move—for now and for all time.

Part I

Become Heart Focused

1

Tools to Soften the Stress

Courage doesn't always roar.
Sometimes courage is the quiet voice at the end of the day saying,
"I will try again tomorrow." [1]

– Mary Anne Radmacher, artist and author

Let's carve out some *you* time by working with a few supportive heart tools that will help you ease stress and open your heart during this time of change. Bring these tools with you every step of the way as you travel through the heart-of-your-move journey.

Tool #1: Writing to and from the Heart

Throughout this book—including at the end of key chapters—you'll find a set of questions intended to encourage you to reflect on what your heart may be telling you during your relocation journey. Several questions are specific to a chapter's landmark concept; others appear in each of the chapters.

By answering these questions, you tap into the power of reflective writing to have a conversation with your heart. Sometimes you'll find the conversation flows, like visiting with a trusted friend and expressing your deepest thoughts. Sometimes, though, the writing might feel strange and uncomfortable, more like meeting a new acquaintance and feeling unsure about it.

Lesléa Newman has written about this feeling of discomfort in her book *Write from the Heart.* She confides, "Your writing is bound to make you uneasy at times, for it calls on all your emotions, especially if you're writing from the heart. You can do it. You are strong, brave, and powerful, even if you feel weak, scared, and small."[2]

Taking time to write *to* your heart and *from* your heart is essential to gleaning benefits from your move—and especially important to making relocation an expansive experience. Answering questions in writing requires understanding of your thoughts and emotions at a deep level. As Julia Cameron wrote in her book *The Right to Write,* "We should write because writing brings clarity and passion to the act of living."[3]

What happens when you're able to reach in and touch your spirit through writing? It enhances your sense of who you are, thus boosting your self-awareness and your self-esteem.

When addressing these questions, if writing right on the pages of this book doesn't feel right to you, consider some alternatives. You can record your answers in a separate journal, include these exercises along with your regular journaling activity, type your answers into a document on your computer, or even express them in some musical or artistic way. Heidi, an artist, fashioned a sketchpad to answer these heart questions with colorful drawings. Choose the style that feels right to you.

How will listening to your heart be a helpful tool as you face your relocation?

Tool #2: Connecting with Your Inner "Moving Mentor"

Imagine that you have within you a loving, caring, wise moving mentor. Let her be your confidante. Have her speak to you about ways to respect the human side of your move. You could even give her a special name!

Rebecca, a mystery writer, named her own moving mentor Nancy, inspired by the fictional character Nancy Drew, and visualized her as a young detective alert to clues that would solve the mystery of the moment. Nancy, the inner moving mentor, encouraged Rebecca to face her moving challenges with a spirit of adventure and discovery.

Rose, an engineer, grew up in a family of four brothers. Many times, she wished she had a sister to share her ups and downs in life. She even wondered what it would be like to have a twin sister. So Rose decided to call her mentor Iris and imagined her to be her twin sister—a sibling who would always have her best interests at heart when going through her move. When the stress of moving tugged at Rose's heart, she took a moment to ask, "What would Iris do to alleviate this tension?"

Elizabeth faced numerous fears concerning her move from her home of forty years to the retirement center in another city where her son and his family lived. She decided that her inner mentor was named My Fearless Angel. This evoked spiritual support and counterbalanced the trepidations she knew she'd experience during and after her move.

When Phyllis learned about the concept of an inner moving mentor, she immediately thought of her real-life mentor, her strong and decisive late aunt. Imagining Aunt Jean standing right by her side directing her through the details gave Phyllis comfort and confidence.

Whether you give your own moving mentor a name or simply tap into your inner wise woman for encouragement, you are honoring the heart of your move in a meaningful way.

Describe your inner moving mentor. What does she like to do? How can she support you? If you prefer, give her a name that resonates with you.

Tool #3: Tapping into Your Courage

Do you recognize that courage is one of the heart tools in your moving toolbox?

According to www.yourdictionary.com, "courage" refers to "the attitude of facing anything recognized as dangerous, difficult, or painful, instead of withdrawing from it."[4] Yes, dealing with managing a move from one place to another is a courageous act.

I was surprised and touched to discover that the word courage comes from the old French word *corage,* which means heart and spirit. No wonder I like that word! I think of courage as an enduring quality a woman possesses throughout the journey of her move.

Many women find courage to be an effective source of strength throughout times of intense change. "I love that my courage is my friend during times of uncertainty or difficult transitions," says Sandra Ford Walston, a courage expert and author of *Courage: The Heart and Spirit of Every Woman*. "There is no need for me to run from myself. My courage permits me to be innately motivated. In courage, my life expresses my heart's core."[5]

At any point in your moving journey, you may feel overwhelmed and wonder whether courage has abandoned you. It has not. Always know that the courage to face your move continues to live within you.

To recognize the reservoir of courage you have within you, describe how courage can be your ally going forward.

Chapter Wrap-Up

Another way to nurture your heart's voice is to learn ways to turn your inner critic into your own personal cheering section. The next chapter reveals six strategies for doing just that.

Heart Notes to Remember

- Take time to write to and from your heart. Reflect upon what your heart is telling you about your relocation.
- Sometimes writing from the heart is an easy task. Sometimes the words may not come quite so easily. That is perfectly normal. Don't despair.
- Imagine that you have within you a moving mentor that cares deeply about your well-being. Imagine what she would say that encourages and supports you.
- The courage to face your move continues to live in you.

2

From Inner Critic to Inner Cheerleader

Notice when you are being mentally harsh or critical with yourself, and consciously begin being kinder and more appreciative.[1]

– Shakti Gawain, *Creative Visualization*

In the introduction, I mentioned how I had scolded myself for not settling in as fast as I expected to after my move from the Midwest to the Southwest. I especially remember feeling harsh. That led to blaming myself for not having my moving act together. I questioned what was wrong with me.

Abby Seixas, the author of *Finding the Deep River Within: A Woman's Guide to Recovering the Balance and Meaning in Everyday Life*, noted this self-judging tendency that women experience. Indeed, it's one she learned firsthand after the birth of her second child. As she wrote,

"Women see themselves as not organized enough, not smart enough, not disciplined enough, not efficient enough, not focused enough, not good enough at parenting, at communicating, at relaxing, at making choices . . . not good enough, period. I also now understand . . . that the belief underlying most of this self-criticism is *something is wrong with me."*

The author encourages her readers to shift the question from "What's wrong with me?" to "What's wrong with this picture?"[2]

My shift from *What's wrong with me* to *What's wrong with this picture* occurred when I made the decision to learn more about the nature of human change and apply those principles to my own relocation. Before this shift, my inner moving critic ruled. After it, my new "picture" became a woman who was much more informed about issues of change, who dramatically reduced the amount of self-scolding she did, who lightened up on herself, and who acknowledged that the emotional storms were a natural by-product of dealing with her move.

When Your Inner Critic Rules

If you're all too familiar with an inner critic, you probably won't be surprised to learn that your inner voice seems to be more vocal than usual during your relocation. If you're not usually acquainted with an inner critic, it may be awakening as if from a long nap. It's common to get startled by its unexpected personal attack.

Regardless, your inner critic can definitely increase your stress, dampen your spirit, and prevent you from listening to your heart. It's one big roadblock!

Of course, it's easy to investigate ways to silence that inner mean girl. I can't tell you how many times I've read and heard suggestions on how to banish, get rid of, or destroy one's inner critic. But for me, the idea of a purging negativity through applying a negative approach feels ironic and downright uncomfortable.

So instead of banishing your inner critic, explore ways to use it as a tool for listening to your heart. Here are six strategies that will help you unmask your inner critic. In doing so, you will promote a greater understanding of what your spirit may be whispering to you.

Strategy #1: Rephrase the inner critic statement into an encouraging statement.

Your inner critic thrives on making statements that are negative, stressful, or worrisome. To take the focus off your critic's negativity, take action to tune in to your inner cheerleader. Create declarations that will give your cheerleader reasons to chant her support.

The process is threefold. First, acknowledge your critic by writing out an inner moving critic statement. Next, turn that negative point into an encouraging assertion. In taking positive steps, you will discover the power to turn down the volume on the inner critic and provide the inner cheerleader with new statements that nourish you. Brainstorm actions that will help make those supportive statements happen.

Examples:

Jody's inner critic statement:

- I'm never going to make new friends like the friends I'm leaving behind.

Jody's cheerleader statements:

- I will take the lead in making new friends who will help me enjoy my new city.
- My friends always tell me I'm fun to be around and I'm a great listener, too.

Jody's support plan ideas:

- Write down in my journal several places and situations where I met my current friends.
- Ask my friends and family for ways to connect with others.
- Join organizations where like-minded people hang out.

- Making new friends takes time. Encourage myself to be patient.
- Keeping in touch with my buddies from my previous community will be helpful as I transition ahead.

This three-step process will help you turn your critic's statements into encouraging ones. Let's try out one example of your own.

Write your inner moving critic statement here:

___

___

___

Now write your cheerleader statements of encouragement:

___

___

___

Jot down several action plan ideas that would help support your encouraging statements.

___

___

___

Strategy #2: Peek behind the inner critic's mask to reveal any blocks to new opportunities.

Occasionally, my inner writing critic challenges me with a litany of needling questions like those mentioned in the introduction. "Carolyn, what do you think you are doing, adding all these heart exercises and activities to your book? Women in the middle of moving madness barely have time to read, much less write about it. This is a ridiculous idea!"

If I had given in to the inner critic's opinion, then it could very well have stopped me from my goal of completing and publishing this book. At least you have the evidence in your hands that I'm not buying into that critical statement.

Nor did Ramona. Her inner critic voice kept telling her to be satisfied with the status quo. "Stay put. Don't rock the boat. You should be happy with the life you've got." Instead, she peeked behind the mask, stared these messages in the face, and looked for hidden opportunities.

She knew if she'd listened to her inner critic, she'd never have mustered the courage to change jobs and move to another city. But wonderful things happened in her new environment. Within two years after her move, she met her future husband at a Habitat for Humanity event. Ramona's ability to see what possibilities lay behind her inner critic's mask served as a way of removing the blocks in her path.

Is your inner critic making statements that block you from achieving your goals about your move? If so, what do you hear? List the nonsupportive statements here.

Is the inner critic really trying to express any fears about this move? If so, what might those fears be?

How might you address your concerns so you can embrace the opportunities and achieve the goals associated with your move?

____

____

____

Strategy #3: Call her bluff and ask, "What's your evidence?"

Your inner critic may be guilty of thinking in terms of all or nothing, evidenced by statements that start with "I'll always . . ." or "I'll never . . ."

What's going on? Your inner voice may be telling you something that's basically irrational, void of reason. It isn't necessarily so. *It's now time to call her bluff.* Demand to see or hear the evidence to support these statements. Turn the irrational into rational.

Before her move, Vanessa heard her inner critic voice say, "You'll never find another house as good as the one you have now. Good luck with that!" So she challenged that statement. When she considered the evidence, she acknowledged that she was actually fortunate to be buying in a buyer's market in her new community. As she widened her search to the suburbs, she discovered lots of excellent choices for her new home.

Vanessa realized that her reluctance to say goodbye to her current home sugarcoated her judgment about it. Truth be told, if she stayed there, she would change several things about her current home.

Is your inner critic making statements that reflect all-or-nothing thinking? If so, what are those statements?

____

____

____

What evidence supports and/or refutes those statements?

____

____

____

What options might lie between the all-or-nothing choices and still work well for you? Perhaps you have a completely different creative idea to consider. Jot down your thoughts and consider a full spectrum of options.

____

____

____

Strategy #4: Send your inner critic on vacation or to the spa!

One day while attending a writer's conference, I heard an author describe how she squelched her inner critic. At the time, an insight popped into my head. What about approaching my inner critic in the *opposite* way?

Now, when my inner critic goes into overdrive, I shower her with lavish and wonderful things in my mind! Instead of imagining locking up that inner critic, why not send her off on a five-star vacation—or at least tell her to get a relaxing massage.

So my negotiation goes something like this: "Okay. I just need a couple hours without interruption. I've decided to send you down the street to the Elizabeth Arden Red Door Spa for a relaxing manicure, pedicure, and massage. Lucky you!" Fortunately, she's always receptive to my Queen-for-a-Day imaginary gifts. (Now, you need to know my inner critic isn't the only one who has all the fun. From time to time, I send myself off to a spa for special pampering after accomplishing my writing milestones.)

When my inner critic keeps bugging me, another approach I've taken is to declare that I'll park her grievances for twenty-four hours and give her permission to bug me all she wants *tomorrow*.

Instead of an argumentative and stressful "No! No! No!" response, I talk to that inner voice with a calm "not now" response. Much better.

If you wanted to encourage your inner critic to stop bugging you, what would you do? List a few options here. It's okay to be silly and have some creative fun!

___

___

___

Strategy #5: Take the edge off perfectionism and control.

One of my most stressful relocations involved moving into a home that required several pre-move house improvements. Despite how meticulous I was about getting "excellent" references for home contractors, we still experienced ridiculous mishaps that were completely out of our control.

I'll spare you the full collection of my woes, but I'd like to share one example. I was very impressed with how our granite installers used the inside of their large truck as a workroom, thus containing the dust created by their saws. Unfortunately, on the fourth day—the one and only day I did not personally supervise—the installers brought their equipment into our three-car garage. The result was a thick, messy layer of dust that covered everything in that space.

I've seen enough HGTV home improvement shows to know that unexpected incidents lurk in most home improvement projects. Regardless, I can be quite a perfectionist and a control freak when it comes to organizing these kinds of projects.

Being a perfectionist and trying to maintain a controlling hold on things can take different forms. Psychologist and researcher Randy O. Frost identified dimensions of perfectionism, which include setting very high personal standards, being concerned about making mistakes, doubting one's ability to accomplish a task, and placing a high importance on things being organized and orderly.[3] Hmmm—thinking back to the previously mentioned incident, Frost's descriptions sound pretty darn familiar!

Hara Estroff Marano believes that perfectionism stifles risk-taking, creativity, and innovation. "It is a steady source of negative emotion," she shares in a *Psychology Today* article. "Rather than reaching for something positive, those in its grip are focused on the very thing they want to avoid—negative evaluation."[4] For me, the negative evaluation was self-imposed. In addition to stressing out about the incidents themselves, I continually questioned my own ability to hire good people and make good decisions.

Upon later reflection on this episode and others like it, I would be happy to have a do-over that involved less personal stress and more positive perspective. For example, after reading *Moving: The Challenge of Change,* I counted my blessings when I learned of a woman whose moving mishaps exceeded my own. When her moving van arrived at her new home and parked on a steep incline nearby, the driver stepped out to check his position. The brakes failed and the van rolled down the driveway and slammed into the kitchen![5]

If you want to preserve your sanity, I suggest that, to the best of your ability, you put perfectionism aside while in the midst of a move. Let's be honest. You simply can't control everything and trying to do so will cause your stress level to skyrocket. It's a huge price to pay. The next time my ability to control goes out the window, I'm determined to put into action some tips from my fellow female movers:

- Keep your eye on the big picture. Are you focusing too much on the details?
- Ask yourself, "How will I feel about this tomorrow, next week, next month, next year?" (This is one of my favorite stress busters.)

- Have a trusted friend on standby (in person or by phone) with whom you can share your woes—and later toast these new life experiences.
- Remind yourself, "This too shall pass." Encourage the belief that you'll get through this challenge.
- Embrace the art of slow, relaxing breathing.
- Ask yourself, "What's the worst that could happen?"
- Take a few moments to walk away from the situation, collect your thoughts, and formulate a strategy for facing it anew.
- Explore the source of the stress. Talk to those involved. If needed, consider changing plans. (I wish I would have changed our painter after repeated no-shows.)
- Tell yourself, "I'm doing the best I can today."

What positive supportive techniques could you use when your perfectionist tendencies are causing you stress? List them here.

____

____

____

____

Strategy #6: Create affirmations that support you now.

Many women consider the use of affirmations an excellent way to help them face the stress of a change. The website www.freedictionary.org simply defines *affirmation* as "a statement asserting the existence or the truth of something."[6] An example would be "I am a courageous woman who is confident and happy."

Cindy called using affirmations a godsend when it came to her move. "Creating statements that support 'the ME I am today' as well as 'the ME I want to become' is a strategy that has shielded me against the stress of my move."

I find it interesting that I'm not much of an affirmation kind of gal—until I'm facing a tough challenge. Then when I make affirming statements that fortify my spirit, they help me smooth the rough waters of my transition. A few of the affirmations I used during my last major relocation are:

- I know that change includes a few surprises, and I'm prepared to face those with confidence.
- I treat myself like I would a best friend.
- I care about my health and well-being as I go through this relocation.
- I acknowledge the feelings that pop up during this change and express them in a respectful way.
- I am open-minded about change.

Take a look at the last affirmation, "I am open-minded about change." Despite my expertise in the human side of change, I must admit, change isn't always easy for me. So my belief about being open-minded about change was important for me to instill in myself.

Also, notice that my affirmations are worded in the present tense. I avoided saying that "I *would like to be* open-minded about change." I also didn't say, "I *will* be open-minded about change." I certainly don't want to take the negative approach and say, "I don't want to be closed-minded about change."

Instead, affirmations work best when they're stated in a positive way using the present tense to declare the essence of what's happening now. Heidi, my client who loves to draw, even created an affirmation poster that hangs in her office. It features an affirmation done in calligraphy and includes a drawing of a colorful garden of flowers. She actually added her cat, Tiger, who peeks around one of the flowerpots. Her affirmation is: "I trust my new path. I believe in me."

Create two positive affirmations that support you right now. Be sure to write them in the present tense. You can create affirmations that express a current strength you wish to emphasize or an area you'd like to manifest.

Affirmation: ______________________________

____

____

Affirmation: ______________________________

____

____

Sybil used her love of inspirational quotations as her launching pad for developing affirmations. She identified several of her favorite quotations that touched the areas she wanted to affirm during and after her move. Then she created a statement using those areas that motivated her heart.

Sybil's Examples:

Original quotation:

> *"Kind words can be short and easy to speak, but their echoes are truly endless."*[7]
>
> *—Mother Teresa*

Sybil's affirmation:

> *I support and uplift myself and others with my kind words.*

Original quotation:

> *"If you had to choose only two qualities to get you through times of change, the first should be a sense of self-worth and the second a sense of humor."*[8]
>
> —*Jennifer James*

Sybil's affirmation:

> *I daily find ways to smile, giggle, and laugh.*

Jot down an inspirational quotation and affirm the aspects of the quote that inspire you.

Original Quote: ______________________________

____

My Affirmation: ______________________________

____

How often should you say your affirmations? Danea Horn, the joyful gal behind creativeaffirmations.com, suggests that you say your affirmation five times in a row, three times daily (morning, noon, and night). "The more we hear something, the quicker we believe it," Danea shares.[9]

When I was in the throes of moving, I chose to begin and end my day with my affirmations. I said them at least three times in a row, usually while looking in the mirror during my facial skin care routine. And when I noticed any moving stress surfacing, I'd interrupt myself, take a break, and repeat them at any point in the day.

Think about a frequency that could work for you and give affirmations a try. How often (e.g., three times a day) and when do you plan to state your affirmations (e.g., when I wash my face in the morning, as I eat my lunch, and before bedtime)?

How often?

When?

Where?

What routine might it be a part of?

For those of you who write or draw out your affirmations, where might you post them?

Affirmations have been like mental anchors that remind me of the *me* I want to manifest. When I acted contrary to that, my inner moving mentor would offer reminders in a gentle, caring way. "Am I treating myself like a best friend? What can I do to show that?" And when I caught myself demonstrating actions that reflected my affirmation, it would always make me smile. "Good for me," my inner cheerleader would say.

An affirmation opens the door.
It's a beginning point on the path to change.[10]

– Louise L. Hay, *Experience Your Good Now!*

Chapter Wrap-Up

Now that you've turned your inner critic into your personal cheerleader, you'll be introduced to four more exercises in the next chapter that further encourage you to listen to your heart.

Remember, taking time to complete these exercises will buffer some of the surprises and challenges of your relocation . . . and soften the stress.

Heart Notes to Remember

- Rephrase the inner critic's words into a statement of encouragement.
- Peek behind the inner critic's mask to reveal blocks to new opportunities.
- Call her bluff and ask, "What's your evidence?"
- Send your inner critic on a vacation or to the spa!
- Take the edge off perfectionism and control.
- Create affirmations that support you now.

3

Listen to Your Heart Exercises

In our deepest moments of struggle, frustration, fear, and confusion,
we are being called upon to reach in and touch our hearts.
Then, we will know what to do, what to say, how to be.[1]

—Roberta Sage Hamilton

How do you begin a conversation with your heart? By responding to probing questions that resonate with the emotions that come up around your move. This chapter includes four written exercises that invite you to start thinking in a heart-focused way.

Consider giving yourself time to relax into your thoughts after one exercise before doing the next. Percolate each heart conversation and see what insights come up for you. You might do one exercise a day for four days or one exercise a week, as some of my clients did. It's up to you.

You'll see that some of these exercises are more appropriate if you haven't moved yet. If you've already moved, feel free to modify any of these activities to fit where you are now in your relocation journey.

Exercise #1: Wise Woman

To acquire knowledge, one must study;
but to acquire wisdom, one must observe.[2]

—Marilyn vos Savant

Imagine that you have a dear friend who's going through a relocation. She seeks your wisdom on ways to help her deal with her trying times as she leaves a place that's familiar to her and as she starts fresh in a new environment.

What advice would you give your friend who is in the middle of a move right now?

Next, review your words of wisdom. What ideas could you glean that relate to your move? What words and phrases support you now and may soften your relocation stress? Jot down your ideas here.

Exercise #2: Moving Memories

It doesn't matter if you've moved a lot, a little, or not at all—your memories are likely to have a powerful influence over your approach to the move you're now considering, the move you've decided to make, or the move you've just made.[3]

– Audrey McCollum, Nadia Jensen, and Stuart Copans,
Smart Moves: Your Guide through the Emotional Maze of Relocation

My memory of moving before my senior year of high school entails so much sadness. In contrast, my memory of moving to Tucson after my husband and I were married is filled with so much joy and a sense of hope.

The process of looking back before looking ahead enhances your life and honors the past. You'll find meaningful insights and observations percolating from such remembrances.

Take some time to think about the moves you've made in the past. What have you learned from previous moves? What worked well? What didn't work well? What would you do differently? What insights come up? Jot down your thoughts and feelings here.

Exercise #3: Fears of Moving

Whenever we take a chance and enter unfamiliar territory or put ourselves into the world in a new way, we experience fear. Very often this fear keeps us from moving ahead in our lives. The trick is to feel the fear and do it anyway.[4]

—Susan Jeffers, *Feel the Fear and Do It Anyway*

Going through any major change can open the floodgates of our emotions. And prime among them are fears.

Even *after* the move, new fears may appear. That's why it's important to identify the top fear about your move that is residing in your heart. Create a face-my-fear plan. If time permits, do the exercises again to target other fears and options for defusing them.

Describe one of your top fears of moving.

____

____

____

____

____

____

____

Determine and state its source.

____

____

____

____

____

____

____

List at least two benefits that may be gained by making sense of this fear.

How can you turn your fear into actions that support you and your goals? Write out a brief face-my-fear plan.

Exercise #4: The Heart-of-Your-Move Intention

Intention is gentle and keeps you in the moment, focused on unfoldment.[5]

—Jennifer Louden, *The Woman's Retreat Book*

What is the meaning of the word *intention*? A quick inquiry with my computer word program suggested a multitude of synonyms such as *aim, goal, target, objective, plan, meaning,* and *purpose.* While the bulk of the words imply strategizing and action planning, it's the last two words that we'll embrace in this exercise: *meaning* and *purpose.*

When developing an intention statement, you are searching for something that has meaning and purpose for you right now. You are probing what your heart is telling you that you need. The following exercise is designed to help you craft a draft of the heart-of-your-move intention. The questions are inspired by an activity I first discovered in Jennifer Louden's incredible book, *The Woman's Retreat Book,* when I sought guidance for planning a home retreat.[6] I found the intention activity particularly helpful and modified and expanded it to reflect our focus—the heart of moving.

Spend a few minutes on each question below. In fact, set a timer for two minutes for each question and write whatever comes to mind. Don't worry about grammar or spelling. Let your thoughts and feelings flow freely.

1. When I hear the word relocation or moving, I feel . . .

____

____

____

____

____

2. What I most yearn for with my move right now is . . .

____

____

____

____

____

3. What really stresses me out about this move is . . .

____

____

____

____

____

4. *What I fear will happen is . . .*

5. *What I hope will happen with this move is . . .*

6. *My dream move includes . . .*

Now look over all your responses. Which ones pop out? What surprises you? What themes repeat themselves? Go back to what you wrote and circle those themes.

Also, what words or expressions resonate as you reread your answers? Underline them so you can easily spot them and think about them.

After reviewing your circled themes and underlined words or phrases, your next step is to use them to help you create a statement of intention. Louden suggests arranging the words into "a positive, compelling, and simple question."[7]

Here is the compelling question I created for my move:

How can I soften the hard edges of my moving experience?

Let me share examples of other women's heart-of-your-move intention statements.

Eleanor:

What do I need to do next to feel more informed and connected to my new community?

Margaret:

How can I best face the loss of my closest friends?

Dee:

What can I do to respect my honest feelings about this move?

Christy's first draft:

How can I not get so overwhelmed and crazy with the details of my move?

Christy read her first draft a couple of times and realized the focus of her intention statement was avoiding a negative outcome. She decided to write a second draft that created a more compelling question to move her to a positive outcome.

Christy's second draft:

How can I encourage serenity during this chaotic time?

Now create your own intention statement. Write it down and keep it handy. Let the heart-of-your-move intention serve as a beacon to light the path ahead.

Hold onto this intention statement as you contemplate the question that your heart values most right now. Reread it when your stress levels intensify. List helpful times to review your heart-of-your-move intention statement.

____

____

____

____

____

____

Chapter Wrap-Up

"Become Heart Focused" was the theme for part I of our book. So far you've developed easing-your-stress tools and you've discovered ways to turn your inner critic into a cheerleader. I hope you've also opened a dialogue with your heart.

"Respect Both the Art and Heart of Your Move" will be our mantra for part II. You'll receive a detailed overview of the true meanings of the art of your move and the heart of your move. You'll learn how these two expressions differ and why it's vitally important to your well-being to bring heart-focused strategies into your relocation plan. Insightful suggestions from our experts will also be given to support you in creating your Stress Reduction Team.

Heart Notes to Remember

- Imagine that you have a dear friend going through a move. Think about the kind of advice you would share with her that reflects the heart of moving.

- Reminiscing about past moves can be beneficial as you face your current move. Glean from the past the ideas and lessons that can help ease your heart now.

- Accept that strong emotions, especially fears, can be a natural part of the change process. Identify the top fears of moving and create a plan to make sense of those fears.
- Creating the heart-of-your-move intention statement will guide you as you search for meaning and purpose associated with your move. Let it serve as a beacon to light the path ahead.

Part II

Respect Both the Art and Heart of Your Move

4

The Art and Heart of Moving 101

The beginning of wisdom is to call things by their right names.[1]

– Chinese proverb

When people learn that I'm an author and consultant whose specialty is the human side of change, they typically look at me with a curious expression and ask, "What is the human side of change? What exactly do you mean by that?" Before long, I'm engaged in a brief overview of the two sides of change and their unique differences.

Here you'll learn the expanded version of the lesson that addresses what is meant by the human side of change—or what I call the *heart of your move*. It's like a two-sided coin in which you experience both sides.

Let's compare and contrast each side of the relocation coin: the *art* of your move and the *heart* of your move. Here is an overview of what you'll do:

- Learn the true differences between the art and heart of moving

- Identify strategies that respect both sides of the relocation coin
- See a graphic analogy of what it's like to get out of balance
- Refer to charts that make the comparisons easy to understand
- Discover different timetables for each approach
- Create boxes for the art and heart of moving

Let's start with the *art* of moving, a concept you may already be familiar with.

What's the Art of Moving?

It's easy to find relocation resources to guide you through the mountain of practical details necessary to complete a move. Look at any book, article, or web page on the subject and you'll see lots of topics on moving.

A few topics you'll find include:

- Where to locate an extensive moving checklist
- How to pack and unpack
- What to consider in selecting moving services
- Where to find an excellent real estate agent
- How to search for the perfect home
- How to get through the financing maze

These topics together form a major category that emphasizes the details of moving. When you step back to catch your breath, you realize it encompasses a monstrous to-do list. These kinds of details and actions fall into the realm of the *art* of moving. Unfortunately, they tend to get all the attention. What about your emotional well-being as you tackle that monstrous and overwhelming list?

What's the Heart of Moving?

Have you noticed resources that support and nurture the emotional side of your relocation—the *heart* of your move—are sorely lacking?

Commonly, women get so wrapped up in the *art* of their move that the *heart* of their move gets pushed aside. Still, whether they like it or not, a few heart moments sneak in. Below you'll find comments and questions that provide clues to the sensitivity of the human side of moving:

- How do I make sense of the emotional aspects of this relocation—how I *feel* about moving?
- I've moved before, but this move seems harder than the others. I feel like I should be on top of this, but I'm not.
- Why do I have strong feelings of loss, especially when this is a positive and highly desirable move for me?
- I'm an experienced organizer and packer, so I don't understand why I still feel overwhelmed and confused.
- I really want to make this move go well, with every moving choice being the right one. Yet, so much is either unpredictable or out of my control.
- Why does it take such a long time to really feel at home in our new home and community?

While the *art* of moving tends to look at moving details as external events to be planned and completed, the *heart* of moving is internal, activating a gamut of emotions and touching your spirit. Why? Because a big move allows you to orchestrate the relocation process at two levels. And by embracing both art and heart, you can begin to clarify your changes while enhancing your personal growth and nurturing your emotional well-being.

Separating the Art and Heart Aspects

Let's separate the elements of change into their components and reorganize them so we can closely examine them. Like putting Humpty Dumpty back together again, this chapter aims to reconstruct your moving experience in a way that makes sense to you.

My move from Missouri to Arizona was difficult. I had moved before and didn't understand at first why this time felt different. But once I separated the two perspectives—looking at the heart of my move as opposed to the art—and examined their differences, I gained a valuable insight. I realized I had done a fantastic job on the *art* of my move but a dreadful job on the *heart* of my move. So it was time for me to call things by their right names and to create a plan with strategies that respected both sides of the relocation coin.

Figure 4.1 lists a few of my *art* of moving strategies.

Figure 4.1
Carolyn's ART of Moving Strategies

- Identify a real estate agent
- Buy a house
- Pack
- Notify everyone of new address
- Move
- Arrange the furniture
- Unpack boxes
- Locate new services (doctor, dentist, insurance agent)
- Get an Arizona driver's license

Share two or three of your own "Art of Moving" action items or strategies.

Now let's look at the other side of my relocation coin—my *heart* of moving strategies. I drafted these action steps after my move to Arizona, and they're listed in figure 4.2.

Figure 4.2

Carolyn's HEART of Moving Strategies

- Learn new information about transitions as part of studying change.
- Meet with my husband each Sunday to discuss transition ideas and apply relevant information to our move as well as relocation concerns.
- Explore ways to honor the challenging losses I felt due to the move.
- Identify ways to connect with the new community and put action items on a schedule.
- Make weekly calls to family members back in Missouri.
- Reconnect with favorite traditions that were enjoyed at our previous home and community.
- Ease up on negative thinking and self-scolding as I settle in. (Cut myself some slack!)

Share the "Heart of Moving" strategies you're already doing or would like to add to your relocation planning.

Did you discern the differences between the art and heart strategies? Do you see how your spirit can be lifted by integrating heart-focused actions into your relocation plan?

Discerning Key Differences

Doing this expanded strategic planning and following through make a big difference in helping you feel less overwhelmed. Yet virtually every moving checklist you'll find today addresses *only* the art of moving, not the heart of moving.

Now please don't get me wrong. I'm not here to give the "art" part a bad rap. In fact, I've included an assortment of art of moving ideas in this book. But I *am* dedicated to giving the *heart of moving* a well-deserved name badge.

Addressing *both sides* of the relocation coin is essential so you can experience as smooth a move as possible.

The Riding-a-Bike Analogy

Before I switched my consulting focus to helping women enhance the heart of their relocations, I worked with executives facing profound change in the workplace. One analogy I used anchored the importance of attending to both the art and heart of a change: the image of riding a bicycle applies perfectly to one's relocation experience. Take a look at figure 4.3.

Figure 4.3
Both wheels in place

Imagine that the front wheel represents the art of your move and the back wheel is the heart of your move. Remember that the *art* of moving handles the details of your move and the *heart* of moving respects the emotions of your move.

Now imagine that the back wheel is flat, has fewer spokes, or is missing completely.

Figure 4.4
Missing the back wheel

I once worked with a hospital administrator who was coordinating a workplace change. I showed him a chart that offered two lists of strategies: the *art* of change and the *heart* of change.

The administrator confidently zipped through the checklist for the *art* of change, quickly checking off the strategies he'd already covered. "Yes. Yes. Yes. Been there. Done that."

Then he glanced at the list of strategies that respected the *heart* of company change. As he scanned it, he sat completely quiet and motionless. At that moment, a fresh realization soaked in. No heart-of-the-change strategies had been considered in the overall change plan. Of course, I was there to remedy that.

By now, you know that my mission for this book is to provide strategies that help you install the *heart* wheel into your relocation plan—thus making it stronger. When you do, you'll have a more balanced approach that provides a smoother ride through your complete relocation journey.

Characteristics Side by Side

Another way to appreciate the differences between the *art* and *heart* of moving is to view their characteristics side by side. Let's take some of those you've learned so far and add a few more. On the following page, figure 4.5 reflects those ideas. Take a moment to review that chart.

When I first placed the pairs of traits onto the original Art-Heart Chart, I began to understand their differences. I originally presented the pairs as one *versus* the other. I could imagine a sports announcer saying, "And it's The ART of Your Move University battling The HEART of Your Move University. Who will win?"

I soon released the sports analogy of art *versus* heart in favor of the concept of art *and* heart. This is a fundamental shift from viewing the two sides as clashing to viewing them as separate pieces of the relocation process that come together. Part of making sense of your relocation is creating a safe and supportive space that encourages the union of the art and heart characteristics.

Yes, there may be times that the art and heart don't get along. Chapter 8, which features The Muddled Middle Heart-Stage, goes into more detail about and presents strategies for the confusion that occurs when the art and heart are at odds with each other.

Figure 4.5
Art-Heart Chart

ART of Moving	HEART of Moving
external situation	internal or personal response
your actual move	how you adjust to your move
details of moving	emotions, feelings associated with the move
filled with specifics	filled with meaning

What else might you glean from the Art-Heart Chart? You may begin to appreciate the fullness and complexity associated with your relocation. You may welcome that insight with the recognition, "No wonder I'm so stressed out!" As you let yourself listen to your heart as you respond to each of the heart exercises, it is my hope that you will discover more and more meaning and purpose in your move.

What other characteristics reflect the art and heart of your move? Add your ideas to Your Art-Heart Chart at figure 4.6.

Figure 4.6
Your Art-Heart Chart

Your ART of Moving Ideas	Your HEART of Moving Ideas
____________________	____________________
____________________	____________________
____________________	____________________

Discovering the Different Art and Heart Timetables

Another point to note is that the *art* and the *heart* of moving have different timetables.

For many, gaining a sense of feeling "at home" (i.e., the *heart* of your move) takes much longer than the time it takes to move and unpack (i.e., the *art* of your move). "Our heads and hearts move at different rates," says Daryl Conner, a psychologist and leading executive change expert. "The capacity that we have to intellectually observe, form an opinion, decide, and act is greater than our capacity to move through the same sequence emotionally."[2]

Some even suggest a time window of two to five years to feel fully comfortable with a change brought into your life. I was sitting in an adult education class taught by a counselor the first time I heard this statistic. I remember shaking my head in disbelief. "Getting comfortable with big change won't take *that* long," I grumbled to myself. But after I experienced similar timetables, I began to pass along that same piece of wisdom.

For some women, the two-to-five-year estimate seems incredible to them, too. "What? Two to five years? Much too slow! Doesn't apply to me!" Diane told me. She's a consultant who specializes in helping professionals with conflict resolution skills. Yet three years after making that "much too slow" declaration, she approached me at a women's networking meeting and divulged that her *heart* transition did, indeed, follow this slower timetable.

For me, this insight that the heart takes longer to really feel "at home" after a move was both a relief and a stress buster. Remember, I had first been tough on myself for feeling unsettled after my move from Missouri to Arizona. My inner moving critic kept scolding me for not having my settling-in act together.

But trying to rush the adjustment of your heart is a lot like telling a newly planted seed to hurry up and grow! Once I learned that this journey could take several years, I lightened up on myself. I replaced my harsh, impatient self-scolding with self-talk that promoted patience and self-care—something I knew I needed to do anyway.

So if you're like me, you certainly have enough external stresses during your move without adding self-imposed judgments to the pile. Encourage yourself to lighten up.

Creating Boxes for the Art and Heart of Moving

When you start packing all your possessions, consider adding two more boxes to the pile, knowing they will come in handy and lift your spirits after the move. One box respects the *art* of moving and the other respects the *heart* of moving.

Open-Me-First Art of Moving Box

Think about the things you'll need when you arrive at your new home. What items do you want to access during the first few days of living in your new home?

For example, we really enjoy watching television, so our Open-Me-First Box had our TV remotes and extra batteries. We also knew we'd be eating a lot of carry-out meals the first week, so we packed paper plates and napkins, plastic utensils and cups, and little packets of salt and pepper.

If you're a coffee drinker, you might pack coffee cups, a coffeemaker, and your favorite blend of coffee. Of course, for your family, you'll want to pack supplies the kids will need right away. And it's a good idea to pack paper towels and toilet paper in your box. You might even place an extra copy of your overall packing list in this Open-Me-First Box.

One of my favorite art-of-moving resources is Martha Poage's *The Moving Survival Guide.* The author calls this special container of essentials her "survival box." She recommends clearly marking your box with instructions—e.g., "open immediately" and/or "place on kitchen counter"—for the movers. Be sure to instruct them to pack this box *last* on the moving truck so it will get unloaded *first.*[3]

Donna Kozik and Tara Maras call their important package

"The Necessary Box." In their book *29 Days to a Smooth Move*, these authors recalled how they organized their lists under headings such as cleaning supplies, kitchen, snacks, tools, and bathroom items. They recommend packing an extra change of clothing, too.[4] Clever ideas!

What items would you pack in your Open-Me-First Art of Moving Box?

Heart ♥ Memo

What Do You Do with Your Most Critical Items?

One of the most common complaints that Agile Life Design coach Ariane Benefit hears from her clients is losing vital papers during the shuffle of moving. Her advice? "Create a single safe place for all your most critical vital documents. You can get a portable safe/document box, a briefcase, or a set of folders. Ideally, your documents container should be fireproof and waterproof."[5]

Here is Ariane's list for the most common essential documents to keep in a special place.

- New house keys
- Bills to be paid
- List of emergency contacts in new location
- List of phone numbers for movers
- List of phone numbers for new services you'll need in your new home
- Passports
- Insurance policies
- Checkbooks
- School transfer information, immunization, and medical records for the kids
- Birth certificates/adoption records/marriage records
- Legal records and papers related to your new home

My Grocery Store

When planning your boxes, list essential items you will personally carry with you. Whenever I travel, I always carry what I call "my grocery store." This grocery store idea started when we packed a few essentials for driving our cars cross-country for our move from Missouri to Arizona.

My "store" is typically a gallon-size see-through plastic bag that holds my travel essentials: energy bar, gum, lip balm, tissues, wet wipes, cough drops, ink pen, glasses cleaner, earplugs, alcohol pads, and a few bandages.

In fact, my grocery store goes into my carry-on bag when I travel on a plane or in a tote bag when traveling in the car or on the bus. When we toured Egypt, for example, one of our fellow tour members slipped while inside the Great Pyramid and scraped his hand. His wife, a retired nurse, was relieved when I reached into my grocery store and offered him an alcohol pad to clean the wound and a bandage to cover it. So glad I could help out.

Open-Me-First Heart of Moving Box

Now let's look at packing a second box that I call the Open-Me-First Heart of Moving Box.

Think about the things that could give you a sense of comfort or relaxation in your new home. Your *heart* box might include photos of your favorite people, a small selection of books, framed inspirational quotations, and/or items that hold symbolic value for you.

For example, Hannah, a recent graduate from the University of Arizona, packed a mug with a photo of her sorority sisters on it. Teresa packed a miniature American flag to display after her move to Europe. Betsy packed three decorative crosses.

An ordinary item may represent a treasure to you, whether you pack it before the move or locate it after the move. Leslie Levine, the author of *Will This Place Ever Feel Like Home?*, suggests that you "create a care package for your soul" by finding "possessions that will help to lessen the pain of transition and turmoil."[6]

Another neat idea she suggested is pulling together what you'd need after the move to enjoy an at-home spa day.[7] Oh, how I wish I'd read this book before my last move!

What items would you pack in your Open-Me-First Heart of Moving Box? Create your own name for this box.

Chapter Wrap-Up

I recall meeting a young real estate agent who told me she was in the audience several years earlier during one of my presentations. What surprised and delighted me was that she remembered the lesson on the *art* and *heart* of moving. She shared with me how valuable those insights had been to her both then and now as she fulfills her role as an agent. An ancient Chinese proverb states, "The beginning of all wisdom is to call things by their right names." This young professional has learned, remembered, and connected with the value of calling things by their right names.

Your ability to distinguish between the art and heart of moving will help you see whether your relocation plan offers a healthy balance. Perhaps, like many women, you may discover that your task list lacks heart-oriented actions. I encourage you to add them. Like nutrition and rest, paying attention to our heart is an essential part of self-care during a potentially stressful time.

In our next chapter, you'll meet professionals whose services can help you balance the *art* and *heart* of your relocation journey.

Heart Notes to Remember

- The *art* of your move involves detailed specifics. It's your master to-do list that has to be created and followed for you to move successfully from one place to the next.
- The *heart* of your move is personal and unique to you. The heart of your move respects the feelings and emotions that surface during your move.
- Both the *art* and the *heart* of moving are important. Like a bicycle with two wheels, each wheel is an important aspect of moving. Consider developing strategies for each of these.
- The time it takes to fully feel settled and at home (your heart timetable) may be much longer than the time it takes to physically move (your art timetable).
- Enjoy creating two boxes that you'll open first when you reach your new home—one for the *art* of your move and another for the *heart*. Make sure your movers leave them accessible when they pack.

5

Create Your Stress Reduction Team

When we join together with others, a powerful force is created. Strong teams accomplish more than strong individuals.[1]

– Jennifer Sellers, Sheri Boone, and Kate Harper, *Pause: 52 Ways to Shift Any Outcome in Less Than a Minute*

One of the most stressful ways to tackle your move is by trying to do it all by yourself.

I suggest finding others to be a part of your pre-move and post-move Stress Reduction Team, or SRT. Even women on a tight budget have creatively found ways to negotiate with others for help in their relocation journey. Emmy is one; she convinced several of her friends to help her pack boxes, luring them with friendship time together and a hot pizza at the completion of the task.

While your friends can be instrumental in providing valuable emotional support during your relocation, professionals can assist you with details that will smooth your move and alleviate some of the stress you feel. Recruit people who respect your feelings and understand the stress you're going through. This in itself provides tremendous support.

Professionals who can assist with your move include the following:

- Real estate agents
- Professional organizers
- Newcomers clubs
- Human resources services and relocation assistance
- Life coaches

We've interviewed experts who have loads of great ideas to help you with your relocation. Let's take a closer look at several of the professionals who might serve on your SRT—those who can assist with both the art and heart of your move. Of course, this is just a sampling, not a comprehensive list. You'll find a worksheet at the end of each section to help you organize your information and make a plan to assemble your team members.

Real Estate Agents

Not only are real estate agents expert in assisting with countless aspects of your relocation, but many believe that respecting the heart of your move is also an important dynamic to consider. One such agent is Sherie Broekema in Tucson, Arizona. I first met Sherie at a National Association of Women Business Owners luncheon after my move and have enjoyed her spirit and enthusiasm. (We've both had the experience of sharing our homes with energetic miniature dachshunds!)

Sherie's commitment to keep in touch with her homebuyers is first rate. Through regular newsletter mailings, friendly phone calls, and special events—like booking an entire theater for her clients to see a Harry Potter movie—she demonstrates her genuine dedication to stay connected after the sale. She's the kind of person you want on your team.

In the last thirty-five years, her clientele has included homebuyers, home sellers, and a niche market of seniors who are downsizing—a population she feels a lot of empathy toward as their moving situations can be particularly difficult. "We agents joke that we should move ourselves every five years so we can re-experience the stress our clients are going through as they age," says Sherie.[2]

An especially tough situation occurs when a senior breaks a hip and can't use the stairs anymore. With reluctance, she realizes she has to move from her two-story house.

Sherie has seen many clients get so caught up in the logistics of the move that they don't slow down and pay attention to the bubble of stress they're immersed in. "Typically, agents give newcomers the names of handymen and carpenters, but they may not know about resources like life coaches to help with the emotional strain," Sherie explains. She sees that kind of coaching and support as an important niche to be filled in communities everywhere.

Symptoms of Stress

What symptoms show up when Sherie's clients get overly stressed? One symptom is difficulty parting with "stuff"—treasured possessions that might have to be left behind. A more serious symptom is blaming others, including family members and even the real estate agent, for having to give up their homes. As Sherie has observed, "Small things go wrong and their emotions go sideways. Feelings of resentment can build. Sometimes they yell; sometimes they're silent and passive. Clearly something is bothering them."

But regardless of the ages of her clients, Sherie encourages them to get involved in their new communities. Specifically, she points them to activity groups for hiking, art, music, and more. She says, "It's part of my job to find out their interests and put them in touch with places where they'll find like-minded people."

Remember, your real estate agent can be a gold mine of information and contacts for you during and after your move.

Real Estate Transaction Stress Triggers

Kelle Sparta, a highly respected trainer and speaker in the real estate industry and author of *The Consultative Real Estate Agent*, provides training and coaching to both new and experienced agents.[3] She encourages agents to build strong relationships with their clients and not to overlook emotional issues clients may face. In fact, in an article for *REALTOR® Magazine Online*, Kelle identified ten "triggers" for real estate transaction stress—that is, reasons people get upset, discouraged, or overwhelmed during the process of buying or selling real estate.[4]

If your own temper flares unexpectedly or your patience wears thin, consider whether these reasons could be at the root of any discontent you may feel as well.

- Things are happening differently than they expected.
- Feeling like they don't have control over the process.
- Not fully understanding the process.
- Not feeling respected (by spouse or real estate practitioner).
- Too many options from which to choose.
- Afraid to make a commitment to buy a home.
- Panic about making the wrong decision/not being able to find home in tight timeframe.
- Not finding the "perfect" home they had envisioned.
- Finance worries.
- Lack of trust in real estate practitioner/mortgage broker/ home inspector, etc.

(Kelle Sparta, "Help Emotional Clients Keep Their Cool," *REALTOR® Magazine Online*, September 2008.)

I would add two more triggers to Kelle's extensive list:

- Reluctance or indecisiveness due to previous bad experiences.
- Not being in agreement with spouse on home-buying and/or home-selling matters.

Kelle recommends that agents prepare themselves for triggers like these by anticipating their clients' concerns and coming up with solutions early on. For example, she tells her first-time buyers that they aren't allowed to panic until she tells them it's time. The buyers laugh and agree. Kelle uses humor to curtail a potentially negative trigger.

Look over the list of triggers again. Which ones are you concerned about? What might you do to soften the stress of that situation?

I'm grateful to discover people like Kelle and Sherie—professionals in the industry who recognize, value, and promote heart aspects of moving. Professionals with that strong combination of skills will be great members of your Stress Reduction Team. Kudos to all those in the relocation industry who respect the heart of a woman's move.

If you're considering adding a real estate agent to your SRT, jot down your ideas below.

Agent's name: ______________________

Agency name: ______________________

Address: ______________________

____

Phone: ______________________

Website information: ______________________

Email information: ______________________

Date of connection: ______________________

Benefits of adding this person to your team

____

____

Questions for team member

____

____

Budget considerations

____

____

Notes

____

____

____

____

Professional Organizers

I've also included professional organizers on my Stress Reduction Team, both before and after my move. Here's another example of just how beneficial this team member can be.

Cynthia, a recently divorced woman, decided to move back to her hometown to be near her family. She first moved into a furnished apartment. With little to move, things went fairly smoothly. However, when she was ready to take the next step—move into an unfurnished apartment in the same community—she wasn't sure how to proceed. Plus, she didn't have the emotional or physical energy to do this monumental job on her own. And members of her family weren't able to assist because of their physical disabilities. Given that she didn't have much energy to do it all herself, Cynthia needed guidance, so she took charge and hired a professional organizer to help her do these tasks:

- Sort her belongings and pack the items she selected for her new place
- Determine where to put any items she didn't want
- Hire a moving company to transfer the large items she did want
- Assist in unpacking so she could quickly get organized in her new home
- Help find and buy the right furniture for her new place

Naturally, Cynthia missed the spacious house she'd lived in before she divorced, but getting her things organized made a big difference. Doing so allowed her to immediately feel better about her new home—and feel optimistic about starting the next chapter in her life.

Benefits of Working with an Organizer

Even if you're not in the same situation as Cynthia, having a professional organizer at your side as you go through your relocation journey will soften your stress. Consider these five benefits:

- As your organizer helps you sort through your belongings, she may encourage you to prune back your possessions before you pack. Because your organizer doesn't have a sentimental attachment to your things, she can offer a fresh perspective and help to accelerate the decision-making process. An organizer will provide guidance when you're choosing which items to bring to your new home and which items you don't need, like outdated paperwork, unpacked boxes from previous moves, and items that no longer hold any special significance.

- Keep in mind that a supportive organizer won't force you to throw away things that you really do wish to keep. If you want it, keep it. Moving is already such a busy, high-stress time; minimize your anxiety and post-move regrets by keeping those items you're unsure about.

- Because you have someone you're partnering with, you don't feel alone. An expert is at your side offering advice about best ways to pack and organize your boxes, selecting the right movers, and more.

- Getting organized before the move means a smoother and faster unpacking process after the move. You'll find it frees up time for what's most important when you arrive in your new location.

- Ideally, you could hire a professional organizer both before *and* after your move—someone who would even assist in room arrangement, furniture placement, and floor plans. (For more design help, also consider interior designers, home stagers, and redesign specialists as smart choices for your SRT. We hired a stager to freshen up and improve the interior of our last home before it went on the market. Our impressive team rallied behind us, and we sold the home in four days!)

Which benefit listed here means the most to you? Why is that benefit important?

Many professional organizers are trained and certified in transition, relocation, and senior moving services. To locate a professional organizer in your area, check out the website for the National Association of Professional Organizers at www.napo.net. If you're a senior considering a move or you're seeking guidance to help an aging parent go through a move, I suggest connecting with a senior move manager who is certified through the National Association of Senior Move Managers at www.nasmm.org.

Choosing a Professional Organizer

When you're choosing an organizer to hire, Sharon Harn of Sharon Harn Organizing emphasizes these two key factors: personality and experience. As Sharon explains, "Personality is important because you want to be able to communicate well and know that the person you're interviewing understands your needs. Also, you'll be spending lots of time together, so you want to enjoy that person's company. Sometimes you'll get a good vibe just doing phone interviews with organizers. That gives you an encouraging start on getting to know their personalities before meeting with them in person."[5]

Experience counts for a lot, too, Sharon adds. "For all the organizers you interview, ask about their experience dealing with needs similar to yours—for example, children's rooms, offices, craft areas, or accessible spaces for those with disabilities. Interview between two and four candidates to find the best one for you."

Also, ask for examples of when they've worked with women who were in situations similar to yours. Sharon shared this example: A dean at the college needed to relocate her family for a short time. Because she was the main breadwinner and also had lots of responsibilities at home, it was difficult for her to find the time to do everything needed for the move. Hiring a professional organizer for that purpose made her life much simpler.

As they went through her home, the organizer kept her focused. If she had done the sorting alone, she would have readily interrupted the process with other tasks or reminiscences about the items. But by having a professional organizer with her, she didn't get distracted from the day's focus.

In this case, the professional organizer also coordinated the move and organized the family's belongings for the movers to pack. Because this family moved to a new home in the same area, the same organizer helped with unpacking, too. Naturally, her client stayed involved in the process and made all final decisions, but because she had an experienced person at her side dealing with copious details, the job turned out to be less time-consuming—and much less emotionally exhausting—than if she'd tackled it herself.

Budget Considerations

Of course, considering your budget is an important step as you explore new services to help you with your relocation. Sharon provided some food for thought regarding fees. Generally, fees vary depending on the organizer, city, or region. So it may be a good idea to get several estimates and references. It's always good to have a consultation with one or two professional organizers before you decide to start working with someone. Normally consultations are done at the home and will last for a specific amount of time. Some organizers do not charge for that consultation time. Be sure to ask.

Professional organizers may charge per hour or per project. When you start asking questions, be sure you know what the quote covers. For those organizers charging per project, that fee may include packing, moving, and unpacking.

Be prepared to answer questions during your research, too. A professional organizer will need to know the particulars of your home before making an estimate. For example, Sharon notes, when it comes to moving them, china cabinets can cost more than garage items. Your professional organizer may quote by square footage or by the number of boxes to unpack.

In addition, some organizers can assist you in moving out the items that will go to others by planning your estate sales, donations, or shipping. You can chose to hire a professional organizer to handle just that portion of the move as well.

A little research ahead of time just might put your budget fears to rest—and gain you the assistance of a valuable professional or two.

Heart ♥ Memo

Five Tips for De-Stressing Your Move

Here are five ways to reduce the emotional stress of moving in the early stages of your relocation journey:

1. Before your move, go through your house several times, allowing yourself to savor memories and mourn for what you're leaving behind. Some people take photographs as visual reminders; others require only a mental remembrance.

2. Whatever emotions emerge as you walk through your house, let them. It's important to express them while feeling safe. If you can let them out in the presence of a supportive person, you likely won't take out any negative reactions on others. And knowing you might experience the good, the bad, and the ugly during this process, ask your most supportive friend to be there with you.

3. Relocation is especially hard if you've lost a partner and are moving away from the home you previously shared together. Consider bringing your loved one's essence with you by moving a few of his or her favorite things to your new home.
4. If you can't bring a treasured item with you and you're mourning its loss, photograph it as a keepsake, but also consider bringing a portion of it if possible. As is the case with most adult children, you might not wish to move your mother's good china to your own home. To lighten the load, you might compromise and take only two place settings instead of the full set. The same could apply to collections, such as thimbles, dolls, or spoons. Keeping one or two of these treasures will preserve the memory beautifully.
5. Start planning early, even a year or two before the move, if at all possible. Spend time isolating small areas in your home and organizing them before the "big job" begins. Sort through your junk drawer, your attic or basement, and your bedroom closets beforehand. The more organized you are before the move, the easier the packing and unpacking will be.

– Sharon Harn, Sharon Harn Organizing

Heart ♥ Memo

If you're considering a professional organizer as a member of your SRT, jot down your planning ideas below.

Organizer's name: ____________________

Company's name: ____________________

Contact information: ____________________

Website information: ____________________

Email information: ____________________

Date of connection: ____________________

Benefits of adding this person to your team

____

____

Questions for team member

____

____

Budget considerations

____

____

Notes

____

____

Newcomers Clubs and Welcoming Groups

When Toni Kane retired to Arizona, she took an active role in the Newcomers Club of Tucson, even becoming its president within a few years.

This Newcomers Club is similar to many across the country that organize activities for members and associate members. Says Toni, "Women join for the activities and stay for the friendships. Mostly, friendships are made while attending small-group activities like bridge, hikes, book clubs, and much more." About herself she says, "I was a special education teacher for forty years. Being the firstborn in my family, I like to be in charge, so I guess that's why I became president."

Like Toni, the majority of members were career women or dedicated volunteers in their previous communities. "Because they've been so active all their lives, they seek a high level of activity in their new city," Toni explains. "We're happy our Newcomers Club provides a structure they can plug in to—and a way to meet others quickly when they first move. As a group, we help people stay vital because we offer something for everyone. We even include spouses in some of our activities!"[6]

If you can't find a similar newcomers group in your new community by doing an Internet search, then ask your real estate agent and check around locally. Groups often advertise their activities through notices in the local paper and at fitness centers, churches, and other public places.

While doing online research for this book, I discovered a website dedicated to helping women become better acquainted with their new neighborhoods and surrounding communities. The Welcome Wagon Social Club of Reading, Pennsylvania, offers "an atmosphere of friendliness, goodwill, and helpful information." In addition to civic and charitable events, the social club provides monthly gatherings, such as a book club, coffee club, "movie daze," walk group, wine and cheese night, and more.[7] Sounds like a lot of fun! With a little effort, you'll find groups like this in your new city, too.

Look for more tips and ideas for connecting in the Harmonious Hellos chapter. And keep your eyes open for fun ways to acclimate to your new life.

If you'd like to explore a newcomers group as part of your Stress Reduction Team, jot down your ideas below.

Newcomers Group: ______________________________

Contact's name: ______________________________

Contact information: ______________________________

Website information: ______________________________

Email information: ______________________________

Date of connection: ______________________________

Benefits of adding this person to your team

____

____

Questions for team member

____

____

Budget considerations

____

____

Notes

____

____

Human Resources Services and Relocation Assistance

When facing a relocation because of career advancement for either you or your spouse, don't overlook possible services that may be available through the employer's human resources department. Transition experts are highly trained to facilitate relocations by key employees, thus providing a smoother move.

Why do organizations contract with relocation assistance services for their employees? Because companies want to keep new and seasoned employees satisfied so they won't leave. And having employees who are satisfied in their jobs and new locations positively affects their employers' productivity and profitability.

To learn what relocation assistance companies do for families who are transferring, we asked Lauren Herring. She owns and operates IMPACT Group, which is both a relocation and outplacement company based in St. Louis, Missouri.[8]

IMPACT Group was founded by Lauren's mother, Laura Herring, who recognized how emotional issues for so many people stemmed from having to relocate. Laura became a pioneer in how to support the overall acclimation of families into a new environment. Today, IMPACT Group has more than one hundred employees and three hundred coaches trained in the company's way of helping people.

How Relocation Assistance Companies Help Employees

Relocation assistance companies provide guidance for families in a number of ways, including these three:

- Reestablishing their lives in a new community
- Focusing on the accompanying spouse who often gets left out but is pivotal to the family's adjustment and happiness
- Coping with things in the new place such as locating critical services

Their goals are accomplished largely through personal relocation coaches assigned to work one-on-one with families on the move.

Employees who receive this kind of relocation assistance feel extremely grateful. Says Lauren, "They call their coach a 'guardian angel' for supporting them through this time of financial strain, emotional stress, and major adjustments. They not only get their practical needs met but also their emotional needs—although not in an overt way. We don't lead with the emotional benefits they'll experience, but that's what's really going on."

IMPACT Group also coaches spouses to build a sense of belonging and identity in their new locations. This allows families to feel more at home and helps them get involved more quickly.

A coach can even be pivotal in helping a spouse find a job by advising on resume writing, doing mock interviews, providing negotiation tactics, and sharing proven job-seeking strategies. Lauren shared an example of when she assisted a spouse in her job search. "One family moved to a city in Kansas that had 15 percent unemployment. Knowing the pickings were slim, the wife still felt it was important to get a part-time job there. So her relocation coach suggested she interview for full-time work and then try to negotiate flexible hours during the interview process. That strategy worked well. Within a month, she'd made a few compromises and landed a good part-time job. Having the coach as a sounding board during this time made a huge difference. The process not only helped her keep an open mind, it also kept her from despair."

Relocation assistance companies typically contract their services with employers, not directly with individuals. Yet it's important for individuals to know these companies exist. Lauren explains: "Quite often people don't know what their options are. They need to find out what their company might be willing to do. Perhaps a company has a policy in place that isn't acted upon very often. Employees can go to their human resources department and ask if the company offers any relocation services. They can also contact relocation management companies and find out what's offered to companies."

Remember that many relocation assistance groups work with companies instead of individuals. Check with your human resources department at work. Find out what services they may be able to provide, such as moving allowance, temporary housing, and spousal career assistance. Jot down your ideas here and then decide whether to add this group to your SRT.

HR Department: ______________________________

Contact's name: ______________________________

Address: ______________________________

____

Phone: ______________________________

Website information: ______________________________

Email information: ______________________________

Date of connection: ______________________________

Benefits of adding this person to your team

____

____

Questions for team member

____

____

Budget considerations

____

____

Notes

____

____

Life Coaches

Ariane Benefit (who offered us some great tips in chapter 4) is a life design coach who has moved thirty-five times herself. In her experience, women in the throes of a move often become disillusioned with their new locations. Once there, they quickly discover that reality differs in a big way from what they expected.[9]

"Moving can be an emotional roller coaster with lots of excitement and anticipation at first, and there are also times when the novelty of the new place wears off and you may feel a deep sense of loss or longing for the home you moved from," says Ariane. "Emotionally speaking, you can feel like you're stuck in a place where you just can't find your groove. You ping-pong between loving some of the new features of your new home and deeply missing some things about your old home."

That's when life coaching can be extremely beneficial. A life coach can help you better deal with stress by acknowledging you'll be under stress from the moment you make the decision to move and start your relocation. That realization in itself softens the stress. "Because moving is a huge time commitment, the first step is to take duties off your plate immediately. If you are moving out of the area, consider resigning your volunteer positions or at least taking a hiatus from them. Minimize the number of appointments you make. Take time for self-care so you can be emotionally resilient during the process of organizing the move, moving, and arriving at your new place," Ariane advises.

When Ariane refers to "self-care," what does she mean? "Extra self-care during times of stress means paying even closer attention to how you are feeling and engaging your support system more often than normal. Because moving naturally results in becoming more emotionally sensitive, it helps to spend extra time doing things you really enjoy with people you enjoy being with, eating food you really love that is also good for you, getting plenty of sleep, and spending as much time as possible in natural peaceful surroundings," she explains.

Tips for Finding New Services

What about when you're faced with the task of finding new personal services, like doctors, bankers, and even hairdressers? For women especially, loyal relationships are quick to form among service providers, making them extremely tough to leave. When it comes to banking, Ariane suggests working with a bank that operates in both your new and old locations so you don't have to undo and redo services like automated bill paying.

To smooth out the change, she suggests making trips to your new community well ahead of your moving date if you can. During these visits, start researching new service providers, developing a list of criteria and questions as you interview.

"Most importantly," Ariane emphasizes, "don't jump at the first recommendation you hear. I did that when I needed a root canal and had a horrible experience. I didn't ask basic questions, like how often the dentist did root canal procedures. Instead, I went to a strange dentist based on one person's recommendation and regretted it."

As someone who's moved thirty-five times, Ariane concludes, "There's a real art to making your lifestyle portable. Moving can be a wonderful opportunity to have a fresh start. Working with a personal coach to assist in making *your* lifestyle more portable is a great way to relieve the stress of the move and simplify your life at the same time."

Have you considered adding a life coach to your SRT? If so, what specific area of your life would you like to target? Coaches offer a variety of specialties, including relocation transitioning, career planning, parenting, or enhancing relationships. Also, do you want to explore group or individual coaching? Jot down your planning notes below.

Life coach: ____________________

Company's name: ____________________

Address: ____________________

____

Phone: ____________________

Website information: ____________________

Email information: ____________________

Date of connection: ____________________

Benefits of adding this person to your team

____

____

Questions for team member

____

____

Budget considerations

____

____

Notes

____

____

Additional SRT Members

Do you see how you can turn to a team of professionals—real estate agents, professional organizers, newcomers groups, employee assistance specialists, and life coaches—to soften the stress of your next move? What other groups or individuals do you believe would be valuable members of your Stress Reduction Team?

Perhaps you recognize the benefit of connecting with a career specialist or personal counselor during this transitional time. Or maybe it's time to add an interior designer or a stager to your team. You may know a friend who has gone through frequent moves and can give you advice or a church leader who can offer spiritual support.

Add one more team member to your SRT. Jot down your planning notes below.

SRT member: ______________________________

Company's name: ______________________________

Address: ______________________________

____

Phone: ______________________________

Website information:____________________

Email information:____________________

Date of connection:____________________

Benefits of adding this person to your team

____

____

Questions for team member

____

____

Budget considerations

____

____

Notes

____

____

Heart ♥ Memo

TEAM KATE:

Long-Distance Support for an Ailing Friend

Besides the professionals you add to your team, you may find certain Internet-based resources invaluable. The following is a story of how Sophie used CaringBridge.org to provide long-distance support to an ailing friend after she moved.[10]

Sophie first met Kate at a business networking luncheon. Sophie suggested they exchange business cards and later scheduled a coffee date to get acquainted at a convenient Starbucks. They soon became the best of friends, enjoying coffee dates nearly every week.

Kate was such a treasure that Sophie frequently referred to her friend as a "joyful spirit."

Fast-forward five years when Sophie faced two difficult challenges. First, her dear friend Kate had been diagnosed with cancer and had recently begun treatment. Sophie, along with a group of Kate's other close friends (who referred to themselves as "Team Kate") had been helping their friend with transportation to and from appointments, walking Wiggles (Kate's Jack Russell terrier), running errands, and providing lots of love and support. The team was inspired daily by Kate's courage.

At the same time, Sophie was struggling to process the recent news of her husband's job transfer, which would require the couple's move to another state. Sophie knew that change can be viewed in many different ways. She also knew that her husband's job transfer represented a great opportunity, especially in light of the current economy. Yet her heart was breaking at the idea of leaving behind her dear friend.

Hoping to explore new ways to help her friend, Sophie called a trusted colleague in the health care industry whose sister received treatments similar to Kate's. Her colleague recommended CaringBridge.org, a free website service dedicated to helping patients stay connected with family and friends during any phase of their treatment and recovery. Patients can create their own web pages, each of which includes a blog where they can document their journeys and where friends and family can post messages of support.

Sophie shared the idea with Kate, who was relieved to hear about this time-effective way to connect with her family and pals. She gave the green light to Team Kate to help set up her account with CaringBridge.org. Within a week, Kate's blog was open for business and she spread the word via email to Kate's contacts with instructions for accessing her web page.

The benefits of this project were greater than either woman could have imagined. Kate later disclosed that taking a little time each day to reflect on her experiences (the good, the bad, and the ugly) ended up being her daily therapeutic touchstone. She also knew that if her mind and body said no to blogging, she could skip that day or ask one of her team members to enter her comments.

Her spirits were also lifted by the words of care, concern, love, and joy from well-wishers.

After Sophie and her husband moved, Sophie continued to regularly post special notes to Kate, grateful in the knowledge that a conduit of care had been created to support her friend.

Kate graced this planet for another nine months. Kate's CaringBridge web page then evolved into a gathering place for words of remembrance and sympathy. Friends and family shared the memories that made them laugh and cry. Several site visitors asked about Kate's dog, Wiggles, and how he would be cared for. One of the members of Team Kate who watched over Wiggles adopted Kate's adorable dog.

Sophie misses Kate. Yet she feels blessed that she crossed paths with this joyful spirit, knowing that her life was enhanced by her time with Kate.

Heart ♥ Memo

Chapter Wrap-Up

We're just about ready to wrap up part II, "Respect Both the Art and Heart of Your Move." Good for you for becoming art-skilled and heart-skilled. As Sophie's heartfelt story illustrates, it's critically important to recognize both needs. Without a doubt, it takes both art and heart work to maintain your balance and well-being as you manage the details that take you to your new home.

The next part of our book is devoted to the three heart-stages you'll experience in your relocation journey. Your goal? To feel peace and comfort in your new home as soon as you can!

Heart Notes to Remember

- Turn to professionals who can assist you with details that will smooth out your move and alleviate some of the stress you feel. They are your Stress Reduction Team.

- Look for emotional triggers and explore what's behind any discontent you might feel during your relocation process.
- Recruit people who respect your feelings and understand the stress you're going through.
- Seek newcomers clubs that will help you get active quickly in your new community.
- Ask your employer or your spouse's employer what company-paid assistance services might be available to help with your move.
- Take time for self-care so you can be emotionally resilient during the process of organizing the move, moving, and arriving at your new place.
- Explore Internet tools and resources that support the heart of your move.

Part III

Discover the Three Heart-Stages

6

Heart-Stages Overview

Your mind may be keeping busy with all you have to do before the move, but how's your heart coping? If you're anything like most of us, it's doing its share of flip-flops at the thought of moving. It's important not to pack your feelings right along with the fine china.[1]

– Donna Kozik and Tara Maras, *29 Days to a Smooth Move*

How do you begin to make sense of the changes and "flip-flops" that come to light during your relocation? By learning the essential phases of your transition and discovering new strategies for each step. The heart of your move consists of these three heart-stages that resonate with the emotional sides of your relocation journey:

Stage 1: Gracious Goodbyes

Stage 2: Muddled Middle

Stage 3: Harmonious Hellos

We can predict with a high level of certainty that you'll experience all three heart-stages. Yet what is unpredictable is the degree and intensity of difficult emotions you may feel, the number of unexpected challenges, and the length of time spent dealing with the challenges faced in each stage.

Don't despair. You can turn to this book as your guide as you work through the steps to make your experience more heart focused.

The aspects of your move that touch your spirit are unique to you *and* to each woman facing a relocation. The three heartfelt stages are universal themes that have the potential to strengthen a woman's courage and resolve during her move. You'll increase your understanding of these heart-stages as they apply to you in the upcoming three chapters.

Each dedicated chapter encourages you to interact more deeply with the emotional nature of your change. Heart questions are sprinkled throughout. Reflection and self-care questions conclude each chapter. All are designed to help you listen to your heart and soften your "flip-flops."

For now, here's a quick overview of the key destinations during your heart-of-moving journey. Figure 6.1 features a visual showing the signposts for the three heart-stages.

Figure 6.1

Three Heart-Stages of Your Move

Gracious Goodbyes

Once the decision is made to move, the mind enters a *goodbye* stage—the first of three heart-stages. Lots of things stop or "disconnect" for you in this stage. It represents the endings that will occur as a result of your relocation. Some endings are insignificant, involving little to no thought; some endings are welcomed; and then some are profoundly heartbreaking.

What can you do to make your goodbyes gracious and respectful when your heart isn't happy with certain endings? That's what we'll explore in the next chapter as you learn ways to graciously say goodbye and acknowledge those endings that mean the most to you.

Muddled Middle

Both lurking between *and* overlapping the *goodbye* and the *hello* heart-stages is a muddled *middle* stage in which you haven't yet let go of the old and haven't yet embraced the new. This middle gap could also be called a bridge of confusion because uncertainty reigns. During this heart-stage, certain things just don't make sense.

"Gee, can't I just skip this stage?" you may ask. Nope. The bridge from *goodbye* to *hello* provides a natural path to take whenever you encounter a major change in your life.

The upcoming chapter about the muddled *middle* stage looks at multiple ways you can learn from the confusion and make sense out of the nonsense that's adding to your stress.

Harmonious Hellos

The third and final heart-stage is the *hello* stage. While you're saying goodbyes and undergoing lots of disconnections in the first stage, in the third stage you're saying many hellos and filling your life with fresh connections. Your goal is to manifest *harmonious* hellos.

This heart-stage represents the new things that will enter your life. It's the phase when you start to settle in with your new home while taking steps to experience harmony, comfort, and an extremely welcome sense of organization. Ah, finally, some order out of the chaos!

Although this particular heart-stage could be considered the easiest for some, a woman can still be vulnerable to emotional setbacks. And even if all is clicking well for you in this *hello* stage, you'll still glean new ideas and strategies in the Harmonious Hellos chapter that can strengthen your new connections.

A Simple—and Not So Simple—Path

For simplicity's sake, the three stages described in this book are laid out in a linear step-by-step-by-step arrangement. Although you know that moving is far from simple, imagine taking three giant steps back and viewing the heart-of-moving path from a broad perspective. From that vantage point, the Gracious Goodbyes generally occur first, the Muddled Middle happens next, followed by the Harmonious Hellos.

Now for the not-so-simple part: It's crucial to realize that your heart has the talent and capacity to participate in more than one heart-stage at once—at any time during the relocation journey. You can even experience all three simultaneously.

Take heart. The more heart-skills you gain, the more strength, courage, and determination you will muster. Yes, personal growth and wisdom can take a creative hold in each and every heart-stage you face. By listening to your heart, respecting your inner guide, and building heart-focused strategies, you'll be able to shift your soul from chaos to comfort.

Chapter Wrap-Up

With that gradual, gentle shifting in mind, let's take an in-depth look at the first heart-stage, Gracious Goodbyes.

Heart Notes to Remember

- The journey of the heart of your move involves three heart-stages: Gracious Goodbyes, Muddled Middle, and Harmonious Hellos.
- Gracious Goodbyes is the first heart-stage of your relocation. It represents the things that will end as a result of your move.
- Muddled Middle is the second heart-stage. This stage signifies the in-between time period when you haven't yet let go of the old and you haven't yet connected with the new.
- Harmonious Hellos is the third heart-stage. This phase embodies the new aspects and new connections associated with your move.
- You can experience two or even all three heart-stages at the same time.
- By learning new skills that respect the heart of your move, you will muster more personal strength, courage, and determination.

7

Gracious Goodbyes Heart-Stage

Great is the art of beginning, but greater is the art of ending.[1]

– Henry Wadsworth Longfellow, American poet

Your initial decision to move sets off a flurry of activities designed to get you into your new home. You might find it appealing to focus on the new place, the new town, or the new job that sparked your move. New, new, new. But when you focus on the *heart* of your move, the first stage actually addresses the opposite of "new." It's the time you acknowledge the important endings that will happen.

After I created an early draft of this book (originally an ebook),

I asked a writing workshop teacher to review my ideas and give me feedback. She suggested I make a tiny but significant tweak to my sentence "Every major change will produce loss." The instructor marked out the word "will" and wrote the word "may" over it, thus changing the sentence to "Every major change *may* produce loss."

Well, after much thought, I changed it back. Experience repeatedly shows that *every major life change WILL produce loss.* You simply cannot insert big changes into your life without something exiting it. The nature of change insists that some things will stay and some will go, therefore some "hellos" will definitely lead to some "goodbyes."

The first heart-stage in your relocation journey that respects the heart of your move is called Gracious Goodbyes. It's when your heart asks you to pause and examine the old. By old, I mean what's familiar and comfortable to you that won't continue.

When people experience a profound change, certain things stop. In fact, a lot of things stop. Some of those things you may welcome. For example, when I moved to Arizona, what stopped for me were the long, chilly winters of Missouri. But I also moved much farther away from my father, so I lost the convenience of driving a few hours up the highway to visit him.

With your move, what endings and losses are you facing? Let's address this heartfelt stage with strategies that acknowledge and honor those losses—ones that aim to respect the dearest things you're leaving behind.

One way to open a dialogue with your heart is to take a closer look at three words that relate to this stage of your transition—gracious, goodbye, and endings. Words come alive through the meanings we instill in them. So let's look at different ways we can define gracious, goodbye, and ending. The inspiration for these definitions is a blend of past experiences, client comments, and my trusty online dictionaries www.yourdictionary.com and www.freedictionary.org.[2]

Gracious Goodbyes Heart-Stage Definitions

Gracious

- Showing warmth, kindness, and courtesy to others (and to yourself!)

Goodbye

- An act of parting or leave-taking; saying farewell
- Separating from a person or place
- Word origin: from the expression "God be with you."

Melissa's thoughts: saying goodbye to things
"Goodbye means saying farewell to friends. I'll miss them so much. I'm saying goodbye to things, too—the gorgeous mountain views out my kitchen window, the wildlife that rambles past my home office chattering their complaints, the warmth of the desert sun."

Stephanie's thoughts: feeling torn
"I've lived in the same house for thirty years. Now that John is gone, the house is too big for just me. I know saying goodbye to my house is a good decision. Yet I feel torn at times. Too many loving memories here."

Mandisa's thoughts: bringing a state of grace to goodbyes
"I know what goodbye means, but I really had to dig deeper with this notion of what *gracious* goodbyes might mean. It makes me think of the word *grace.* I consider that I'm in a state of grace when I bring a state of tribute to my goodbyes. It means bringing forward a spirit of gentleness and self-care as I begin to recognize the things I'll lose with this move."

How would you define "goodbye" or "gracious goodbye" for yourself?

Ending

- To stop (a stopping point)
- To bring to a conclusion, completion, or finish
- A demarcation point or boundary beyond which something does not exist or occur

Marisa's thoughts: upcoming graduation
"Four years at a cool college, an engaging major, great professors, the joy of hanging out with my sorority sisters, and even a winning football team. I now have to graduate and leave all that behind and become a grown-up."

Esther's thoughts: pushed out of my old life
"I moved because of the loss of a loved one. It's heartbreaking to feel like I've been pushed out of my old life with a door slamming shut behind me. There is no way to reenter that life. That's what this ending is like for me."

Carol's thoughts: growing and stretching
"Ending. To no longer do. To have something stop. When something no longer exists even though it did only seconds ago. Some endings you'll love. Some you'll hate. But to grow and stretch, you must leave behind many things."

What does the word "ending" mean to you as you face your move?

Facing the Challenge of Saying Goodbye

How have other women in a situation similar to yours faced the challenge of saying goodbye? I've gathered true-life stories from women who have gone through their relocation journeys. As you read these scenarios, look for similarities in their situations and yours, finding comfort in knowing that you're not alone.

First, let's see how Sally faced the Gracious Goodbyes heart-stage of her move with a few personal observations to follow.

Sally's Move: Saying Goodbye to Coworkers and Friends

After months of anticipation, Sally's husband, John, finally received the good news of his promotion and upcoming transfer from Boston to Dallas. The couple was grateful that the company would not only cover the moving expenses, but would also handle many of the relocation details. Sally felt confident she would be able to find a nursing position in Dallas. Their new financial situation allowed her to take her time exploring her own work options.

Sally's coworkers from the hospital hosted a goodbye party on her last day at work. Her best friend, Harriet, also planned a special celebration at Olive Garden for just the two of them. Harriet took lots of photos and then created a photo scrapbook of their favorite times together. Both women shed tears, gave each other hugs, and shared promises to keep in touch.

Two Types of Goodbyes: Literal and Symbolic

Moving away initiates two kinds of goodbyes—one literal and the other symbolic. There were a number of ways that Sally literally said goodbye: the hospital party, her friend's celebration, Harriet's photo album. Saying your farewells aloud and shedding tears are among the most observable ways to say goodbye.

Some women feel that saying goodbye is the most difficult and painful part of the moving experience. I'll never forget what I saw when my husband and I first moved into our current home in Tucson. The parting owner had literally kissed the window by the front door, leaving her red lipstick "goodbye" mark on the glass.

Another kind of goodbye is more symbolic in nature because it acknowledges that an entire chapter of your life will close. Each page may represent a unique ending.

For example, Sally had served ten years as a nurse and nurse administrator at the community hospital. She and her husband were avid Boston Red Sox fans. They also loved and supported the Boston Pops orchestra and rarely missed the "Pop Goes the 4th" summer event. They felt a strong sense of being Bostonian, making leaving the city emotionally difficult.

For some, the move will be wanted and chosen, like Sally's. She wanted the change that she and her husband had chosen and felt excited about their move. For others, a decision to move often stems from an unwanted event or a circumstance that's out of their control. That's what happened for Deborah. When her husband was transferred from Alabama to California, Deborah got angry about having to leave her sweet Alabama home. "I moved to California kicking and screaming," she said to me when she learned about my coaching specialty, the human side of change.

Ironically, *both* Sally and Deborah would journey through the three stages of the heart of their moves—whether or not they wanted the move and whether or not it was in their control. "I thought that because I wanted to make this move, I could just skip the goodbye stage and that confusing in-between stage, and go right to the 'hello new home' stage," said one of my clients. She called her move a positive decision, yet as time went on, she wondered why she couldn't settle in as quickly as she'd expected.

Heart ♥ Memo

Saying Goodbye to Coworkers

Angela Smith, owner of Accu-Assist.com, shares several ideas for saying a fond farewell to those you care about at work.[3]

- Purchase a special address book to pass around the office and let coworkers add their contact information to it. Be sure there's room for them to leave "goodbye" comments if they'd like.
- Bring your camera to work during your last week and take candid photos of your coworkers while they're working—or

while they're just goofing around. If you go out for a special lunch together, have someone at the restaurant take photos of the whole group.

- If there's a particular item that one of your coworkers often borrows from you (such as a CD, calculator, or reference book), present it to him or her as a gift before you go.
- Leave behind little "surprises" in the desk drawers of special coworker friends so they'll find them after you're gone.

Heart ♥ Memo

The Loss of Identity

Grace's early career spanned more than fifteen years in public school education. She served as an elementary school teacher, a junior high counselor, and a middle school assistant principal. Her education, training, and livelihood defined her identity as an educator. Then an unexpected divorce opened up an opportunity for her to move to a new city and explore another career direction.

Grace moved from San Antonio, Texas, to St. Louis, Missouri, after she accepted a position with an assessment firm to develop skills tests for elementary schools. Grace was confident the transition would be smooth because she'd still be wearing her education hat. Instead, she discovered that her new work environment and private company culture dramatically differed from what she knew. Before long, she felt like a fish out of water in her new workplace.

Barely two weeks after moving into her new town house and after only a few days at her new office, Grace experienced her first surprise at work. At a committee meeting, as her boss gave her an extra assignment to do, he concluded his instruction with this casual quip: "And, Grace, I'm sure you're all settled in now." Without thinking, Grace chuckled under her breath with an ironic laugh and, catching herself, quickly cleared her throat to muffle it. She closed her eyes as she visualized all the boxes strewn everywhere in her new place.

Fortunately, she was at the opposite end of a long conference table so her boss neither saw the surprised expression on her face nor heard her mini-attack of amusement. As the meeting continued, Grace's mind reeled from the inadvertent joke he'd made that only she understood.

Grace's situation and reaction of surprise provide several insights to learn from. One insight examines the common practice of identifying yourself (and others) with what you do. When meeting people for the first time, a predictable and frequent opener for introductions is "What do you do in your work?"

For Grace, her identity had been wrapped up in two roles: being a public school educator and being a wife. Both underwent a profound change at once. Added to the career change and divorce stew was leaving the house and community where she'd spent the previous ten years. It's little wonder Grace was surprised that her new boss's comment seemed surreal to her.

Remember, too, that when emotional endings occur as a direct result of your move, they can manifest themselves anytime during your heart-of-the-move journey. Interestingly, Grace didn't realize that she'd lost a big part of her career identity until after moving to her new situation.

It's easy for friends and family members to share expressions such as *You'll be fine, Just give it time,* or *You'll bounce back.* Perhaps you're saying that to yourself, too! In truth, comments like "just give it time" aren't likely to ease the real losses you're experiencing. No one elaborates on what you are to do with that time you're giving yourself. One thing that helps is to acknowledge and respect those endings. Focus on your heart with these exercises.

Write down three endings you are facing with your upcoming or recent move.

Ending #1: ______________________________

Ending #2: ______________________________

Ending #3: ______________________________

Which ending is the most challenging for you now and why?

____

____

____

____

____

How might you encourage a sense of being "gracious" (warm, kind, and courteous with yourself) during one of the three endings you listed?

____

____

____

____

____

Connections and Disconnections

The word "connection" acknowledges a sense of wholeness and being a part of something larger. It is defined as being joined, linked together, or establishing a bond or close relationship with.[4] The essence of who you are is reflected by the zillions of connections you create each day, each week, each month, each year.

When Jordan brainstormed her pre-move connections—those she had before her upcoming move—she included items like her children's school and related activities, her favorite grocery store just down the road, her dog's helpers (whom the dog considered his personal assistants), being in the same city as her sister, and the panoramic sights of the active city from her living room windows. Figure 7.1 shares her list. Her insights continue on page 101.

Figure 7.1
Jordan's Pre-Move Connections

medical professionals	great views of the city
family nearby	swimming pool at house
children's school	nice-size kitchen
children's activities	large front yard and backyard
place of worship	old windows hard to open
coffee shop	yard crew's weekly visits
tennis club	irrigation system
dear friends	just decorated dining room
grocery store with great florist	pet's helpers and house sitters
office supply store	excellent veterinarian
lots of neat hiking paths	city with a university
relaxing salon/spa	big water bills
shopping center nearby	neighbor's strange sculpture
job, job associates	very small garage
house with lots of built-ins	animal shelter volunteer
networking association	low taxes and low cost of living

Heart ♥ Memo

Helping a Child with Special Needs Face a Big Move: Mary and Sara's Story

My sister Mary is no stranger to moving. In a span of only a few months, she and her husband moved part of the family's belongings to a rental home in a new city where her husband took on a full-time position and moved their daughter into a house in a nearby town.

Moving their daughter Sara required special planning because Sara is a young adult who has Down syndrome and a form of autism known as PDD (pervasive developmental disorder). Sara would be moving into her own supported living housing with two special needs housemates, so the act of moving *and* leaving the nest represented several profound changes for both mother and child.

To help prepare Sara for her upcoming move, Mary created a new story inspired by the Social Story method developed by Carol Gray.[5]

Sara's story provided important statements that reinforced not only the upcoming move but also the new behaviors she would be encouraged to engage in. For example, living more independently meant that Sara would be asked to help around the house in different ways. She would also learn to live with new housemates.

Reading the stories became a way of "practicing" events before they happened to lessen the fear of the unknown. The content of her stories compared Sara's life at home before the move to her new life in her "new special house" after the move. Emphasizing positive aspects of her maturing into young adulthood also became another important theme. In addition to the collection of short sentences about these changes, pictures were taken of familiar and unfamiliar surroundings to make the concepts easier to grasp and remember.

It's been four years since Sara moved and she still refers to her place as her "new special home." Her next big change will be coming soon when Sara graduates from high school. Time for another set of stories.[6]

The act of moving results in those connections coming apart in one form or another (the prefix *dis-* is Latin for apart, away, or removed). When Jordan and her young daughters moved to another state, dozens of connections fell away. The notion that one experiences a sense of disconnection is frequently mentioned in sources that recognize the emotions of change. Indeed, to women going through a relocation, it feels like they're earning a graduate degree in facing and dealing with disconnections.

Jordan's pre-move activity helped her begin to more fully appreciate the big-picture benefits of her Gracious Goodbyes heart-stage. Additional benefits emerged. For one, her life had been so focused on mothering her children and working at her job that this exercise helped her define herself as being more than those two primary roles. Overall, Jordan's losses began to resonate in her heart as she listened to and appreciated her inner communications.

List at least three pre-move connections that are special to you.

Respecting How Others Feel About Endings

Experiencing endings as a direct consequence of your move is a normal phase of the change process. That's why it's so vital that you be in touch with your losses. Also bear in mind that if you're moving with others, you won't share all of the same endings. You can expect that you and family members will experience very different, yet individually important disconnections.

I remember a mother expressing her concerns at a transitions program I attended in Phoenix. The mother couldn't understand why her son was so unhappy with their recent move. "How can you not love living in the Valley of the Sun? The weather is wonderful here. We no longer have to deal with the freezing Colorado winters."

Clearly, this well-meaning mother felt relieved to disconnect with the cold winters (as was I when we moved from the Midwest to the Southwest). But the son's disconnections were different than hers. For him, the cold weather of Colorado meant a great blanket of snow to ski on and vivid memories of spending time with his friends on the slopes.

How might the endings of others in your family differ from your own? How might those differences be acknowledged and respected?

Downsizing and Loss

Family members, professional organizers, real estate agents, and retirement center staff personnel have stories to tell about those who struggle with letting go of their things when they downsize to smaller places to live. Here are three stories of how women experienced a downsizing.

Downsizing When Moving to a Retirement Community

Downsizing is required when seniors move into retirement centers or smaller living quarters in their current communities. If you're in that situation, how do you say goodbye to so many valued possessions you've accumulated over the years?

When you're faced with deciding which item to keep and which to throw away, Ciji Ware, the author of *Rightsizing Your Life,* recommends asking three key questions for each item:

- Do I love it?
- Do I use it?
- Do I have the proper place for it in my new environment?[7]

Although your answers to those questions can guide your decision, understandably the process of letting sentimental items go often takes a toll. "Single ladies in particular tend to get attached to their 'stuff'—their furniture and their collections," says Karen Kovacs, the director of sales at Splendido, a continuing care retirement community in Tucson, Arizona.[8] "One of the biggest emotional challenges when shifting to a smaller space is letting go of treasures."

Karen referred to a ninety-two-year-old woman with no children who faced that dilemma. "She had boxes and boxes of things from her previous home. There were far too many things for her downsized two-bedroom home. She was a meticulous woman and couldn't cope with the disarray of her new place combined with the emotions associated with her losses. I stayed with her and, when she was ready, we began to explore ways to let go of many of her things. I also helped her connect with someone who could sell her most valuable possessions on eBay."

Helping new residents adjust to their new surroundings is important for the staff in retirement communities. Splendido is an example of a community that strives to be "transition friendly" by:

- having social workers on staff to help with adjustments,
- offering programs that fit residents' needs, interests, and talents, and
- "matchmaking" friends through introductions to residents who have similar interests.

If these services appeal to you, be sure to consider similar communities in your area.

Downsizing Due to Job Loss

Abbey's family suffered profound downsizing losses when her husband Jerry lost his executive job after the economy took a downward turn. Jerry had been on the fast track and his boss kept assuring him his job was safe. Yet, still, he got laid off. At first, Abbey felt a sense of shock and disbelief following Jerry's job loss. Then came what she called "the great sadness" for everything they lost.

The couple ended up selling their large home and temporarily moved with their three children into his parents' home out of state. Having made the tough decision to sell the home furnished, they lost almost all of the pieces they'd accumulated as a couple. "I felt like some storm passed through and swept away what had symbolized our life we had built together," Abbey conceded.

"People told me so many 'at least' statements, believing they were helpful to us. '*At least* you still have each other. *At least* you have a roof over your head. *At least* you've got your health. *At least* you're still young enough to bounce back.' Those statements implied that I should be happy and grateful. But the truth was that my heart was breaking in a million pieces."

Abbey eventually rebounded by acknowledging her endings and allowing herself to be authentic with the emotions that spilled forth during that tough time. "I had many a good cry."

Downsizing to a Smaller Home after Children Leave

Betty and her husband George decided to downsize to a smaller home, agreeing this was a good choice for a number of reasons: Their children were grown and off to colleges and careers, their big house took too much trouble and money to maintain, and they were feeling signs of aging. So they chose a new patio home development close to a shopping center, and they transitioned into their new place.

Betty shared her experiences, challenges, and surprises from her move. She also shared her insights about why the downsizing process went relatively well for them:[9]

- Betty and her husband had been in their pre-move house for fewer than five years, so she didn't have a lengthy history or deep affection for the home they left behind.
- Betty is a life coach who works with individuals in the area of goal setting and goal completion. She drew on her own coaching training and techniques to help adjust to their change.
- She and her husband both agreed that this move would be a good decision. They also had each other to share the planning and execution of the move.
- Because they'd considered the idea of downsizing for several years, Betty and George got a head start on pruning their stuff. The children were given ample time to peruse the household furniture and other items, and make a place for their favorite sentimental things.
- The couple had more things than they could fit in their new patio home, so they opted to get a temporary storage unit. However, they made a pledge to review the storage contents at the sixth-month point and set a goal to empty the unit before the one-year anniversary of their move.

Yet even with everything going smoothly, Betty faced several unexpected losses that she lamented after their move. One surprise loss was missing having her grown children stay at their home when visiting them for several days. Their visits were simply richer when everyone could spend leisure time hanging around at their bigger home.

Also, the couple no longer frequented a favorite restaurant because their move put them at the other side of town. They had long known the owners and staff there, feeling like it was the kind of place "where everyone knew your name."

She hadn't anticipated how much she'd feel these losses. Like Betty, you may not be able to predict all the emotional endings you'll experience until well after your move.

Are you moving because of a downsizing? If so, jot down several ideas or insights from the examples given.

Tips to Encourage Your Gracious Goodbyes Heart-Stage

As we let go and say goodbye to our losses, we are released to cultivate new paths. Acknowledging your goodbyes, endings, and disconnections is a gracious gesture that speaks to your heart, demonstrates your authenticity, and opens the door to personal growth. Judith Viorst writes in *Necessary Losses* that "the road to human development is paved with renunciation. Throughout our lives we grow by giving up."[10]

The following four tips will encourage your goodbyes to be gracious during this heart-stage. Each tip is followed by a place to jot down additional ideas.

Tip #1: Acknowledge the endings that may occur as a result of your move so you can foster emotional mending.

What are the challenging losses and endings that will happen because of your move—especially those that touch your heart the most? Earlier in this chapter, we named and examined some of those losses. Now, let's be sure to acknowledge them and encourage your true feelings of saying goodbye. By doing so, you're letting yourself be truthful about what your heart needs. This is one of the most respectful and caring actions you can take.

How might you acknowledge the special endings you are facing as a result of your move? How might you honor your true feelings?

____

____

____

____

____

Tip #2: Write a letter to what you will miss the most after you move.

The idea of writing a letter to something that holds emotional value is not new, although it may be something you haven't done before. As an example, Carrie had her son write a goodbye note to his favorite park down the street. It's where the fourth-grader held fond memories of playing and picnicking near the pond that hosted families of ducks—a special place for him.

Carrie had frequently brought her camera during their outings. Before they each wrote their own goodbye letters, she pulled out her collection of images for them to review together. Mother and son each selected a favorite photo, then they sat at the kitchen table to compose their letters. After completing them, they read the letters aloud.

The mother was so moved by the poignancy of her son's honesty and feelings that she used the same technique to write a private letter saying goodbye to her place of worship. In it, she expressed her deep devotion to her faith and the religious community that had been an important part of her life.

Here are a few questions you might consider as you compose your letter:

What are you saying goodbye to?

___

___

___

What emotions are you feeling?

___

___

___

What special memories are related to it?

___

___

___

Why do you hold this as a special place in your heart?

___

___

___

Why will you miss it?

___

___

___

Tip #3: Create a visual memento of your pre-move home and of your favorite old spots.

One method is to create a scrapbook, photo album, or photo book of your favorite images. Take time to shoot photos of your home and neighborhood, getting lots of shots with you and your family shown in your favorite places.

Explore online services such as Picaboo to help you create photo books, calendars, coffee mugs, mouse pads, posters, puzzles, stickers, magnets, blankets, greeting cards, and more from your digital images.[11]

I first discovered this photo service when I found two picture books at my brother's house that featured a recent trip he and his wife took to Alaska. The cover of the photo book was one of their beautiful shots of a whale lunging from the icy blue waters. Seeing it gave me the idea to recommend similar services to promote gracious goodbyes.

In fact, you can also easily adapt this idea to your upcoming *hello* phase. After her move, Allison showcased her new home and way of life with her husband in a scrapbook that included their favorite pastimes and hobbies. Later, she submitted the scrapbook to the agency where they'd applied for adoption. In addition to telling the agency representatives about their home and how they live, the scrapbook helped show the agency how much Allison and her husband cared about building a stable, loving home.

Before she and her husband moved to Tucson, an artist friend gave Nora a gift of an illustration of their Oklahoma home hand-drawn in ink. Nora enjoyed seeing the artwork and reflecting on the pleasant memories from her midwestern home. She commissioned her friend to draw the two homes she's lived in since that move to Arizona. The entire collection is now displayed on a prominent hallway wall.

Edith also found comfort in seeing an image of her prior home. She had sought out an artist from the local watercolor guild to create a rendering of her home in Columbia, Missouri. Years later she moved to the Lake of the Ozarks area where she found the perfect spot for her favorite watercolor in her home office.

List favorite pre-move things you'd like to capture visually to take with you.

____

____

____

____

What ideas do you have for creating or organizing those images?

____

____

____

____

Tip #4: Spend time with friends. Say meaningful goodbyes to each of them.

Don't wait until just before the movers arrive to start your goodbye visits; give yourself lots of time to savor the experience. This is therapeutic not only for you but for your friends as well.

Jackie remembered her first move as a military spouse and mother of two small children. "Looking back on it, I realize I started distancing myself from my friends about six months before we were to leave. I remember being angry with everyone. I'm sure my coping mechanism thought it would be easier to leave friends if I were angry anyway. Unfortunately, I learned that I missed out on six months of fun and closeness. After that, I vowed to encourage myself and my children to avoid that pitfall."

Consider purchasing a small memento you can give each friend before you move. Camille wrote down on two blank greeting cards different favorite memories of time spent with her close friend Jenny. She mailed one to Jenny before the move and mailed the second just after her move. Miranda found a favorite photo of her and her friend Vivian. She bought matching picture frames so they could each have the same photo and frame in their own homes.

Remember that this part of the heart-of-moving journey can be difficult. Don't pretend that all is okay on the outside if your heart is breaking on the inside. Many women bloggers shared how they cried at the idea of losing their best friends due to a move. Although you can call, text, email, tweet, Skype, visit on Facebook, or even send snail mail and cards the old-fashioned way, it isn't the same as regularly hanging out in person with your close friends.[12]

Be sure to connect with your closest friends several additional times if possible before you leave town. You'll be glad you did.

♡ *Jot down a couple ideas for saying goodbye to your friends.*

____

____

____

____

Heart ♥ Memo

When the Shoe Is on the Other Foot

It's an unenviable challenge when someone dear to you is leaving you behind. How can you support that person and soften the stress and the sadness?

Natalie's Story and Tips

Natalie didn't expect to have a difficult time when her older sister Sophie graduated from the University of Arizona and moved to Atlanta. She and her sister pledged to continue to connect frequently by phone or text throughout the week. But during her move, the older sister found herself overwhelmed with relocation details. Consequently, the number of calls to her younger sister dramatically decreased. Natalie felt sad that her sister was no longer around and was disappointed that Sophie didn't connect with her as often as she would have liked.

The year that followed her sister's move, the tables turned and Natalie moved to Philadelphia. She learned firsthand the crazy effort required by moving and appreciated what her sister had gone through. Remembering how she felt with her sister's move to Atlanta, Natalie made check-in calls with family members on Tuesdays and Thursdays during the week and longer calls on weekends. Natalie's advice is this: "Don't forget the ones you leave behind."[13]

Angela's Tip
To graciously say goodbye to a friend or family member who's moving away, consider what Angela did. A close friend was moving to a state where Angela had previously lived so she gave her friend a personalized "Top 10 Must See" list for the new state—a welcome goodbye gift.[14]

Heart ♥ Memo

Chapter Wrap-Up

This chapter explored ways to encourage yourself to be gracious with goodbyes that happen because of your move. Be gentle with yourself as you face challenges with each new ending. Keep in touch with those who can support you. As this chapter wraps up, you'll find additional heartfelt questions that help you better understand what the heart is saying during your Gracious Goodbyes. You'll also be prompted to consider self-care strategies.

The next chapter will help bridge the gap between the goodbyes and the hellos of your move. You'll discover great ideas about and tips for navigating through the middle phase of your journey: the Muddled Middle Heart-Stage.

Heart Notes to Remember

- Endings, losses, and goodbyes are all a natural part of going through a move. Lots of things will stop. Many disconnections will occur.
- Goodbyes are gracious when you show warmth, kindness, and courtesy to yourself and others.
- Endings can be literal or symbolic. An example of a literal ending is saying goodbye to friends. Symbolic endings happen with things in which you have instilled meaning and significance. A symbolic ending respects that this relocation is concluding a whole chapter in your life.
- Identifying the endings that are happening due to your move will help you appreciate the fullness of your losses. And in doing so, you'll not only be moving away but you'll be able to move on. It's the first step in honoring your heart's nudges.
- Although most of the goodbyes happen at the beginning of your moving journey, you can experience endings anytime before, during, and after your move.
- Don't forget to spend meaningful time saying goodbye to friends before you move. Let those close to you express their own goodbyes to you, too.

Reflections for Gracious Goodbyes

What is there to write if it doesn't come from the heart?[15]

– Rachel Ballon, *The Writer's Portable Therapist*

What is your heart telling you about the endings, losses, and goodbyes happening with your move? The questions below will help you reflect on your Gracious Goodbye stage. Doing so validates your true feelings and encourages mending so you can graciously move on.

Remember, these questions are for you alone. Of course, it's okay for you to share your responses, but only if you feel comfortable sharing and if you're with people you trust.

♥ A chapter of your life is coming to a close. Do your best to describe the meaning of that here.

____

____

____

____

____

____

♥ What are some literal endings that might occur as a result of your move? How do you feel about those endings?

____

____

____

____

____

____

- What are some symbolic endings that are happening because of your move? List them here.

- Contemplate the idea of being gracious with yourself as you face your endings. In what way can you show warmth, kindness, and courtesy to yourself and others? Jot down your ideas here.

- Additional notes about your Gracious Goodbyes heart-stage

Self-Care Strategies for Gracious Goodbyes

Moving is inherently stressful. The following questions encourage you to seek new ways to soothe the stress. Pick at least one question to write about here or in your heart journal. If time permits, select additional questions to contemplate. (You'll see that these questions come up again at the end of the other two heart-stage chapters.)

- *Courage, confidence, self-esteem. Which of these needs a lift right now? What action can you put into place over the next day or two to boost your spirits?*

- *What is your heart communicating to you right now? Relay the conversation here.*

- Remind yourself of the importance of self-care. What can you do to strengthen your mental, physical, or spiritual health?

____

____

____

____

- What one step, regardless of how small, can you take to soothe your relocation stress?

____

____

____

____

- Your inner moving mentor is calm and relaxed. She has some words of wisdom to share with you today. What does she say to you?

____

____

____

____

- What other self-care ideas or thoughts would you like to note here?

____

____

____

____

8

Muddled Middle Heart-Stage

It's not so much that we're afraid of change or so in love with the old ways. It's that place in between that we fear. It's like being between trapezes. It's Linus when his blanket is in the dryer. There is nothing to hold on to.[1]

– Marilyn Ferguson, American writer, editor, and publisher

Uncertain? In a state of topsy-turvy? Experiencing a cup of chaos? Welcome to that confounded, confusing, in-between heart-stage of your relocation journey called the Muddled Middle. The bad news is that confusion is a necessary visit along your heart's route. The good news is that you can take that cup of chaos and distill it into a gallon of clarity.

Strong emotions can bubble up during any point of your relocation. Still, the Muddled Middle heart-stage tends to add an extra layer of confusion. This part of your heart's journey is the bridge that overlaps your Gracious Goodbyes stage and your Harmonious Hellos stage. As you enter this in-between stage, you may still be reeling from the losses of the first stage.

Being pulled away from so many familiar and comforting aspects of your life as you move into this middle stage can be disconcerting, even filling you with fear. From her book *Do What You Love, The Money Will Follow,* Marsha Sinetar wrote about such fears when she reflected on her memories of facing a profound change. "I was afraid to cross uncharted, unconventional waters to get to a more desirable place in life, afraid that—when truth be told—I would not have the requisite strength and competence to accomplish what I so dearly wanted." The apprehensions of confronting a new path and questioning her strength and competence led to an initial reluctance to let go. "My mind clung so desperately to the familiar," the author admitted.[2]

Change expert William Bridges elaborated about this in-between stage that seems to be rarely acknowledged but commonly experienced during one's transitional process. "This isn't a journey from one side of the street to the other," Bridges contended. The middle phase—which he calls the neutral zone—is a "time when necessary reorientation and redefinition are taking place."[3]

This chapter explores the uncharted waters of this confusing middle period. In it, you'll learn about the "whats" and "whys" of the confusion that commonly occurs during many moves. You'll also find insights and tips to help you through your Muddled Middle heart-stage and help you lighten up as well as you can. Plus you'll glean ideas from others who have traversed this territory before you.

First, let's look at a few definitions.[4] You might even circle the words that resonate with your own experience.

Muddled Middle Heart-Stage Definitions

Muddled, confused

- uncertain, addled, confounded, perplexed
- a state that causes one to be unable to think with clarity, certainty, or understanding
- thrown for a loop, feeling emotionally derailed
- feeling that something just doesn't make sense

How do these definitions apply to your relocation journey? They all describe the stew of emotions that often flare up during this middle stage. What causes such emotions? That differs for each person. Let's look at how Donna, Belinda, and Joyce each experienced this middle phase.

Donna: pulled in different directions

"This middle phase was tough for me. Sometimes I felt like I was the rope in a game of tug-of-war being pulled in different directions. It was challenging for me to focus. I thought the confusion would go away after the move, but I still felt pretty unsettled for a while even after we unpacked."

Belinda: dramatic change in routine and lifestyle

Belinda believed her feelings of confusion and uncertainty came about because her routine and lifestyle had been dramatically altered when she moved from the hustle and bustle of Washington, DC, to a casual, easygoing environment in Maui, Hawaii.

Joyce: just too many to-dos

Joyce felt extremely overwhelmed with the ton of moving details she had to handle. She found herself with too many urgent "to-do-right-away" tasks that she couldn't seem to prioritize. With so many decisions to make, she admitted to worrying about making the wrong choice.

Describe the confusion or uncertainty you are experiencing with the middle phase of your move.

____

____

____

My own experience: a tough move during high school

I vividly remember one of my previous moves the summer before my senior year in high school. Our family relocated from a small rural town in Indiana to the outskirts of metropolitan Kansas City. My high school changed from a modest countryside place where everyone knew everyone to one of the largest high schools in the state of Missouri where no one knew my name.

My heart ached for my Indiana pals while my head tried to make sense of the drastically different environment. Honestly, it was one of the most difficult memories to relive. My saving grace was heading off to college the following year and moving into a freshman dormitory. There, just about everyone was on the same playing field. We were all the new kids on the block.

Feeling Torn Between the Old Life and the New

Emma described her Muddled Middle heart-stage experience as feeling torn. "Part of me wanted to hang on to my old home and my old life. Part of me wanted to reach out and embrace the new home, city, and life. It was a terribly confusing time for me."

Zarina offered her view about this confusing time. As a result of an unexpected divorce, she moved from a four-bedroom house on an acre lot to a small one-bedroom apartment. Although she was determined to make a happy home for herself, she knew this radical change wouldn't be easy. She explained it this way: "Sometimes I feel like I have one foot in my previous life and my other foot in my new life."

Other women have had similar experiences, including Alice, who calls it a zone between the "pre-move you" and the "post-move you." Chances are good that you'd feel perplexed, uncertain, and maybe even "not yourself." In fact, if you were a car, you'd feel like you were out of alignment. In this chapter's opening quotation, Marilyn Ferguson refers to this zone as "being between trapezes" as if you're caught suspended in midair, feet dangling.

How Disrupted Expectations Affect Us

Daryl Conner, PhD, author of *Managing at the Speed of Change* and a consultant who works with corporations going through profound change, refers to a situation called *disrupted expectations*. When people face a major change, they each have a mental picture of what they expect the change to look like after it's in place. When the expectation doesn't match up or falls short, a personal disruption occurs and can cause feelings of disappointment, discouragement, and confusion. It's common then to begin doubting your own judgment, *especially* if it's a change you chose with much thought and deliberation.

Dr. Conner wrote, "Again, it doesn't matter if the event is interpreted as positive or negative. The important thing is that you are unprepared for the confusion, disconnection, disenchantment, and anger, or even the enthusiasm, joy, and pleasure that is to follow. It's not the surprises in life that are so debilitating. The truly crushing force is being surprised that you are surprised."[5]

I can readily relate to being taken aback by feeling surprised. After my move to Tucson, I was bewildered at my own inability to handle what I considered a simple move. I reacted to that "surprise at being surprised" by being hard on myself for not handling the move well.

I was also surprised at my difficulty transitioning through the relocation. I was even surprised when I learned later on from

Dr. Bridges that this response to change was actually normal. Yet even though disrupted expectations are common, they're still tough to take.

Jean Marie, Ellen, and Amanda faced disrupted expectations as a part of their relocation journeys, as their comments reveal.

Jean Marie: cold hands and cold feet

Although Tucson can have cold weather spells in the winter, the frosty days don't usually last very long. During one of our unusually chilly afternoons, I met Jean Marie while browsing in a clothes shop. She and her family had just moved from San Diego, and they were unprepared for such temperatures in her new community.

"I thought it was supposed to be hot here in the desert," she said, shaking her head as she looked over the small display of sweaters. Her surprise and frustration were honest reactions to her new winter reality. (Several years later, I was astonished when our desert community was hit with multiple days of frost. I'm happy to report our orange tree survived and has finally recovered.)

Ellen: slower adjustment than anticipated

Ellen was completely caught off guard after she and her husband, Tom, moved to an active retirement subdivision home in a different state. Tom needed to be persuaded to make the move and reluctantly accepted the change. However, after they relocated, Tom made new friends right away and was quite happy in their new community.

Ironically, Ellen, the original champion for the change, found herself discontented. That surprised her. Experiencing her own version of a disrupted expectation, she assumed she'd be contented and settled in much sooner than Tom. She also believed she'd be needed to provide comfort and support to an unhappy husband. Instead, developing friendships and feelings of community happened more slowly for her than for Tom.

Amanda: to the other coast and back

Amanda and her family moved from Oregon to the East Coast when her husband took a new coaching position at a private college. Despite their high hopes, his job and work environment just didn't work out. Within nine months, they moved back to Oregon.

"In the time it takes to have a baby, we moved to the East Coast and then back to the West Coast," Amanda confessed with a smile. Although it was no laughing matter at the time, she's now able to comfortably reflect on the experience and its outcome. Her husband even got hired back at his previous employment, much to their satisfaction and relief.

It's true. Sometimes we can transition through the disrupted expectations; other times we have to realize that the new place simply isn't a fit and move on.

Disrupted expectations can occur in any situation of change. You've probably experienced this before; when you relocate, it's likely you will go through some degree of disruption again. Use the heart exercises below to explore your experiences.

Write down a memory of a disrupted expectation in your past. It may or may not be related to a relocation.

What emotions did you feel—surprise, disappointment, etc? How did you respond to these feelings?

How did you express your emotions? Did you share your situation with a friend, spouse, counselor, or other person? Did you explore other means, such as artwork, music, or writing, of expressing your feelings?

____

____

____

____

Think about what you learned from that disruption. Jot down any ideas, tips, or techniques you would like to remember and use again the next time you experience disrupted expectations.

____

____

____

____

Facing the Paradox of Change

A paradox is like a container holding two differing things that may feel contrary, contradictory, and puzzling. During times of huge change, it's easy to feel like you are a living example of paradox, stuck between two opposing worlds—the life you had before and the life you're entering. For a window of time, echoes of those two worlds come together and compete for your attention. That's why this heart-stage is aptly named the Muddled Middle.

After my move from Indiana to Missouri, it actually took several years to acknowledge feeling I belonged in my new state. When people asked me where I was from, I would default to "Indiana." You see, although my body was in Missouri, my heart was still in Indiana. Fortunately, I grew to love Missouri in time and even chose a university in the Show-Me State for my undergraduate degree in education.

Martina: feeling orphaned

Martina remembered several major changes she faced as a teenager. Her father moved the family shortly after her mother passed away. The bond between mother and daughter can be a powerful force. After losing her mom, her home, and her friends in a short time, Martina felt like an orphan. She yearned to make sense of her confusing emotions.

For Martina, the opposite forces of being a daughter to her mother and feeling orphaned by her mother swirled in her heart as she transitioned into a new life.

In her book *Motherless Daughters,* Hope Edelman described how her heart felt after losing her own mother. She wrote that "my train had suddenly derailed . . . depositing me in an unfamiliar country without a map or a ticket home."[6]

Yes, profound changes in life can make us feel completely derailed and mapless. It's no wonder we seek a new map or ticket back home again. That's why it's important to find graciousness in our goodbyes, mindfulness in our Muddled Middle experiences, and a sense of comfort at every stop along the way.

Have you ever felt as if completely opposite emotions were competing for your attention? Share your thoughts here.

Find Your Blanket of Stability

Despite unpredictable challenges that might surprise you, you can soften the stress of this Muddled Middle phase by using strategies you'll find in this chapter. You can face this confusing, perplexing time in a way that respects and honors the heart of your move. And you can discover that this middle void offers the potential for feminine ingenuity and creative cleverness.

One way to move from Muddled Middle to Mindful Middle is to find your blanket of stability. How? By taking time to pause from the chaos of your change and recognizing what is not changing. Can you identify the threads of stability that weave together the old and new elements of your life? Identify several powerful aspects of your life that you can count on—that you can depend on—before, during, and after your move. Like Linus in this chapter's opening quote, we need to get our blankets out of the dryer so we have something to hold on to.

Your values, meaningful relationships, and support of loved ones represent important anchors during your storm of change. In her book, *Will This Place Ever Feel Like Home? Simple Advice for Settling In After You Move,* Leslie Levine wrote that "your anchors make you authentic, your own person with a destiny to choose. Whenever you leave familiar surroundings, you carry with you the inherited wisdom of your past."[7] Linus had his security blanket as "something to hold on to," his anchor. What is the equivalent for you that carries on the wisdom of your past?

For Christina, her "something to hold on to" was both literal and symbolic. When she and her husband decided to move from New Hampshire to Las Vegas, they sold their beautiful Victorian home along with all their furnishings. The one special item Christina did bring on the cross-country drive was her bed pillow. This pillow represented something that wouldn't change—something that continued from the old to the new.

Brooke's blanket of stability was her focus on family. "One approach that I took with our military moves was to remind myself that the move was only temporary. What was *not* temporary, however, was my number one priority of focusing on our family and supporting my husband with his service endeavors."

Heart ♥ Memo

Meg's Pets

When Meg Files, the author of *Write from Life,* and her husband decided to move to Guam, they both felt strongly about bringing their beloved pets—three dogs and four cats! Despite braving a snowstorm to get to the Denver airport for their flight out and tolerating three months of quarantine for the animals once they arrived on the island, it was definitely worth the trouble. Meg's new island routine included a daily visit to her pets until they were released to their new home. Three years later, the couple took the whole menagerie back to the States. "It was so worthwhile to have them there," Meg said, acknowledging that their dogs and cats are anchors that belong to the family wherever they live.[8]

Here are additional examples of anchors or "blankets of stability" for three women:

- For Tara, an executive with a large architectural firm who was transferred after a merger, her strong values and faith were unshakeable during a storm of change.
- For Lupita, the love and support of her family and extended family remained steadfast.
- For Jessica, the fact that she would be able to continue to use her creative talents as a graphic designer was critical.

♡ *Linus had his blanket as "something to hold on to." What are your "blankets of stability" during this time of high change? Write down at least two or three of your top choices.*

____

____

____

Heart ♥ Memo

Transplanting Memories from Your Past to Your Future: A Daughter's Story

Note from Carolyn: Another way to face the Muddled Middle phase created by profound change is to bring pieces of the past into the future. This gesture can preserve a sense of family history and provide comfort. I discovered a heartfelt example of this from my virtual assistant Angela Smith.[9]

On May 22, 2011, a massive tornado struck my hometown of Joplin, Missouri, leveling a third of its homes and businesses. I was relieved to learn that my mother and grandmother were not injured as they huddled together in the hallway during the terrifying storm. However, their house sustained extensive damage inside and out.

In addition to the structural damage, much of the precious landscaping was destroyed. The graceful pink dogwood that had shaded the front lawn for over sixty years had been hurled to the ground, along with every other tree in the yard. Most of the mature shrubs and plants had been torn, twisted, and uprooted. What a sad sight to behold.

The property's landscaping and garden had been a source of great pride to my father, who had passed away seventeen years earlier at the age of forty-seven. In the preceding years, my family had enjoyed spending time together in the yard—playing Ping-Pong on the deck, roasting marshmallows in the fire pit, and catching lightning bugs on the lawn. After my father's untimely passing, my family cherished even more the special outdoor space he had built with his own hands. The lush gardens and meandering rock paths became something of a living legacy, with my mother dedicating much time and effort to maintaining them.

After the tornado, my mother and grandmother moved into a nearby duplex apartment, eventually selling the property to a developer who would repair it and resell it. As the closing date approached, my mother and I spent several days in the blazing August heat digging up various plants and moving them to a "recovery garden" at the new apartment. Our efforts seemed almost futile as many of the plants suffered badly from the extreme summer drought. But only a few weeks later, new growth began to emerge from the daylilies, hostas, irises, ornamental grasses, and creeping phlox—a testament to the resilience of living things.

These special plants will have a few years to recuperate before my mother retires and moves them with her to a new house. Although our family's home can never truly be replaced, we all take comfort in the knowledge that we are bringing an important piece of our family's past into our future.

—Angela Smith, daughter

Heart ♥ Memo

Turn Chaos into Clarity

The opposite of feeling confused about something is feeling clear about it. Clarity can come about when we become well informed about a situation that's important to us. For Rosa, the clarity surfaced when she researched everything she could get her hands on about her new city, Indianapolis, Indiana.

For others, like Lindsey, clarity comes after taking a taste of the life she thought she wanted. Lindsey envisioned herself being a screenwriter in New York. She discovered an extraordinary eight-week screenwriting program in the Big Apple and signed up for it. After her return, she admitted that she was surprised just how much she appreciated her hometown of Albuquerque, New Mexico, with its slow pace, gorgeous mountains, and open skies.

I remember when my husband first broached the idea of moving to Tucson, Arizona. First, I jumped for joy. (Yes, literally! I dislike cold midwestern weather and adore warm weather.) I soon realized that the only thing I really knew about Tucson was that it was located in the hot Southwest desert. We decided to take an exploratory trip to gain information and experience the area firsthand. I was ready for an adventure.

Although it would be a couple of years before our move, this early visit provided a critical introduction to our new community.

Once we arrived, we knew a bit about getting around and where some of the basic amenities were located. We even discovered some of our now-favorite hangouts, like the frozen yogurt shop that we still frequent. If you visit Tucson, be sure to check out Sundaze Yogurt.[10]

Here are more examples of turning chaos into clarity.

Annie: life coaching

Others have gained clarity by connecting with professional life coaches or counselors. Annie felt blessed that she had signed up for a life-coaching program to seek guidance about some of the confusion she faced with her move. "The timing was perfect. I had a caring and competent professional in my corner to help me sort out and address some of my concerns. She really listened to me." The clarity came from Annie's mindfulness and connecting with others she trusted.

Bridget: seeing a counselor

Bridget's mother admonished her for seeing a counselor after she moved. "My mother told me I was crazy to spend money on such a thing. She said that moving is just a part of life and I should just deal with it and get over it. Obviously, I needed a more encouraging voice. For me, the conversations with my counselor helped me with my inner transition and gave me confidence and new skills to face it."

My own experience: creating a pocket of life that's organized

When I was in my forties, I recall experiencing overwhelming change with a new job, new home, new city. I was in my office taking a moment to gather my thoughts for the afternoon's activities when I suddenly found myself clearing out my top middle desk drawer. I emptied all the items, wiped down the inside of the drawer with a damp paper towel, then began to neatly organize the pens, pencils, stapler, paper clips, and memo pads.

At the time, I didn't know what compelled me to do that. Upon reflection, I realized I was yearning to have at least one little pocket of my life that was organized, stable, and predictable. In her groundbreaking book *The Artist's Way*, Julia Cameron wrote, "When the search-and-discard impulse seizes you, two crosscurrents are at work: the old you is leaving and grieving, while the new you celebrates and grows strong."[11]

Heart ♥ Memo

Military Mom, Chief Morale Officer

Note from Carolyn: Lynn remembers her plans to help her children shift from Muddled Middle to Mindful Middle by being more informed about and active with their moves. She describes her memories of multiple moves while her husband, Andrew, was serving as an officer in the Navy. [12]

While Andrew directed the mechanics of the move, I served as officer in charge of morale. The emotional part of moving was the hardest for us, and I took morale very seriously. Our first move from the East Coast to the West Coast was when the children were preschoolers, so there wasn't the angst of fitting in at a new school.

As they got older, I involved them more in each move. The first thing was to talk about *where* we were moving. We'd look at maps and consult almanacs about the weather. I always subscribed to weekend newspapers and got brochures from the Chamber of Commerce for our new home. For the kids, it was interesting to know what people did there for fun. Were there museums? a beach? playgrounds? What sort of sports did kids play? What did the new city have in the way of libraries, shopping malls, and McDonald's?

I also believe it was helpful for my son and daughter to help pack their rooms. They needed to be able to voice what was to be left behind to give to Goodwill and what would be essential at our new home. Later, when we moved from California, the children were to select what toys, books, and clothes to pack in the car to have until our shipment arrived at the new house. When we moved to the Philippines, they each had to decide on that one thing to bring on the plane that helped them feel safe and happy.

How might you turn some of your moving chaos into clarity? What is one thing you might do/read/research or one person who might provide you with some answers or guidance?

____

____

____

Creating Bridges from the Old to the New

How do we create bridges from our old life to our new one? For my consulting clients, I devised a homework assignment that's proved insightful in this regard. This bridge-building activity also aims to help clients make sense of some of the confusion that occurs in the middle of a move as well as give them a window into their inner guidance. (You'll find more detailed instructions for this activity after Hillary's and Miranda's examples.)

In the first step the client draws a picture that illustrates her in the PRE-move situation. Next, the client draws a picture showing how she envisions herself in the POST-move situation. The final step is to slip a sheet of paper between the two, and then imagine the bridges that she wants to build between the old and the new. Also, clients are encouraged to interpret and tweak the activity however they wish.

Hillary's bridges

Hillary's pre-move situation was a cramped apartment near the university with noisy neighbors. Her tenant codes did not even permit her to have flowers at her door. In the post-move situation, she yearned to have her own home with space for a garden in a quiet and safe part of town. She imagined her home as a haven from everyday chaos and stress.

On Hillary's middle sheet, she drew four simple line bridges. Each bridge listed a strategy she felt would help her cross through the middle phase of her move. For example, one strategy was to "leave work at work." Another was to "meet new neighbors early, prevent problems." Her love of gardening popped up on one of the other bridges. "Get involved. Explore garden club and park committee opportunities."

Miranda's bridges

Although Miranda's move was to a nearby community, she still experienced the surprise and confusion of the Muddled Middle heart-stage. She chose to expand the assignment by first sketching out her drawings, then later writing in her journal a narrative describing her illustrations and the insights she gained from the activity.

Her pre-move drawing showed a stressed-out female face with hands of others tugging at ropes pulling her in four different directions. Sprinkled around the drawing were questions marks. Her post-move picture showed a mirror with a peaceful, smiling face enjoying her happy reflection and that of her partner. The words "calm" and "self-care" rested comfortably to the left of the mirror. One hand held another. "These are helpful hands," Miranda wrote, "as opposed to pulling, tugging, and tension hands."

For the middle-of-the-move sheet, Miranda reflected on the very concept of bridges. She drew out three different types. The first one was a long walking bridge made of rope that hung over a deep chasm. At the base of the chasm was a gentle flowing creek. Although the view was the most peaceful of her bridges, the height and shakiness of this bridge rendered it the most frightening. (Miranda admits to a fear of heights.) She wrote that she would have preferred to leave the bridge behind and walk down to the valley below.

Her second drawing, a long suspension bridge, also felt scary. Even though it was much sturdier and offered beautiful coastal views, it still crossed over troubled waters.

The third bridge represented a country covered bridge. This one would be the easiest for her to traverse and with the least amount of fear. Miranda discovered the irony of the last bridge—though being the least scary, it was completely devoid of views.

"Of course, walking on *this* bridge would mean I would miss seeing everything that was around me!"

Miranda percolated on which bridge and what strategies would help her get closer to her post-move vision. She selected a teal pencil, which she considers a relaxing color, and made another sketch. In this image she drew herself flying and jotted down words that would help her soar toward her new life: sing, write, dance, exercise.

Working through this exercise reassured Miranda that she could indeed move successfully from her pre-move to post-move vision—as long as she allowed herself to tap into her natural expressiveness. Miranda's bridges couldn't be built of checklists and agendas. Her crossings would be strongest if she constructed them using visual and physical creativity.

Let's explore this activity now by applying it to your own relocation. After you've completed the three-sheets instructions, you'll find new questions to help you soothe some of that Muddled Middle stress and confusion.

Try out the Creating Bridges activity for yourself. Here are the steps to follow. Remember to feel free to tweak the exercise as you wish.

1. Start with three sheets of blank paper.
2. Create an illustration of your life before the move and title it *Pre-Move Me.* (Relax. Don't worry about your drawing skills. I promise you Art Police won't arrive at your door!)

3. Create another new illustration of your life (or how you envision your life) after the move and title it *Post-Move Me*.

4. Now set the illustrations side by side with a blank piece of paper between, placing the *Pre-Move Me* drawing on the left and the *Post-Move Me* on the right. You could title the center paper *Middle-of-the-Move Me*. Some of my clients like to lay out the middle sheet with the long edge of the paper at the top and bottom, thus giving them more room for their bridges.

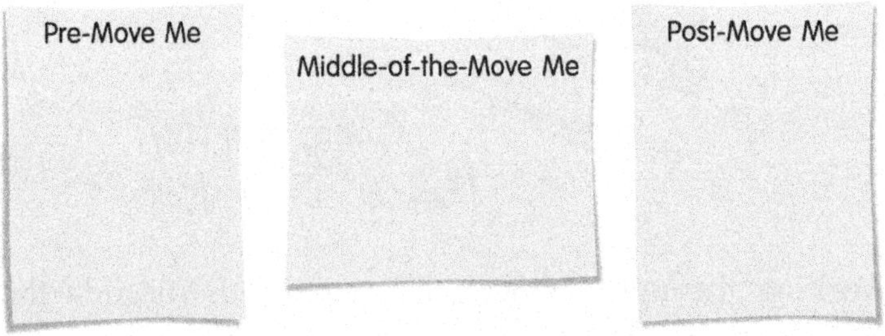

5. Stand back and look at your two drawings. Imagine the bridge that would connect the two drawings. In fact, you could draw a series of bridges on that middle page. What do your bridges look like? What steps or conditions need to be in place to create the *Post-Move Me*? Sketch various ideas about what would work for you. Be sure to include heart-of-moving ideas.

6. Once you have drawn the middle bridge images, spend a little time reviewing all three illustrations and jot down further thoughts below.

What insights did you gain from this activity? Any surprises?

____

____

____

Name at least one Middle-of-the-Move Me activity you can do in the next few days to create a smooth transition between the old and the new.

____

____

____

Jot down a few self-care ideas to make sure you address during your transition from old to new.

____

____

____

____

Heart ♥ Memo

Social Media Tips for You and Your New Job

Note from Carolyn: Using social media also creates bridges from the old to the new. At the time of this writing, one of my personal assistants graduated from the University of Arizona and headed to California to work for a technology firm. I asked Alexa to share a few social media tips for those of you who are moving as a result of a new job. [13]

- Be sure to find out if your new employer has any policies in place regarding social media networking.
- Keep social networking communications with coworkers positive and upbeat.
- Give yourself plenty of time to decide whom you want to be more candid with as you post your comments. Some women prefer not to "friend" fellow workers.
- Use common sense and caution as you decide whether to make your postings public or private. Keep this in mind as you weigh what information you post about your move, home, and job details.

—Alexa Kiel, social media specialist

Identify One Change That Serves "The New You"

You may be surprised to learn that there are silver linings in all those clouds of confusion. These proverbial silver linings represent a special opportunity to let your creative juices flow.

What do I mean by this? Times of high change can be an ideal opportunity to reassess how things have been working for you—or *not* working. When so-o-o-o many things are changing at once, why not explore a few more changes that will yield high personal gains?

Trust me—I'm not proposing change for change's sake. Instead, I suggest identifying things that no longer serve you or haven't worked for you in a while. Now is the moment to have fun and explore new ways, new approaches, new choices. Here are a few examples.

Rachel: choosing a new apartment

Rachel, who loves cooking and baking, found herself in a dilemma with high electric bills due to all the indoor cooking. Additionally, the stove and oven would heat her small apartment to the point of being unbearable. Because she lived in the Southwest's desert climate, opening a window for a cool breeze was rarely the solution.

With her lease about to run out, the timing was perfect for Rachel to explore new apartment complexes. She selected a unit with an outdoor grill and benefited by the nearby trees that provided extra shade. Not only has the outdoor cooking helped her keep her costs down, but she's also expanded her culinary skills.

Mary: trying out new churches

Mary grew up in rural Missouri as a preacher's kid with a strict upbringing from her parents. After high school graduation, she headed to the University of Central Missouri to begin her studies in psychology. Mary added one more change to her transition of moving away from home. She opted to visit a different church each Sunday.

This exploration encouraged her to experience a diversity

of services, ministers, and religious cultures. She settled in at a Methodist church where the minister gave his inspirational sermons without notes. She also noticed other college students at her favorite 11 a.m. service, which in time led to new friendships.

Look at the Big Picture Through Moving Milestones

What's another way to make sense of and clarify the Muddled Middle stage of your relocation? Consider crafting a Moving Milestone Map. Make a list of the major milestones associated with your own relocation. That might include selecting a real estate agent, listing the house, giving notice at work, packing boxes, and creating new heart-stage strategies. Think of ways to be creative in making your list and checking off completed milestones.

I created a milestone roadmap on the inside of a manila folder. Then I used small heart stickers to mark my completed milestones. My transition clients enjoyed approaching this assignment in their own creative ways. Elsie created a mind map. Susan sketched out a timeline continuum.

It's fine to note those important art-of-moving markers, but don't forget to include heart-of-moving milestones, too. You're wise to create a balance of both. Pamela drew a tree with different branches that represented art and heart aspects of her moving milestone plan. Be sure to select several of your milestones that will receive special recognition once completed.

Liz's milestones: a balanced map

Liz's decision to leave Tulsa and return to her native West Coast felt like a "no-brainer" at first. Besides the opportunity to spend time regularly with her aging father and extended family, Liz looked forward to a fresh start. She had weathered a difficult divorce and was eager to be in a home that wasn't full of bittersweet memories. Liz knew that her daughter, Tina, would also benefit from having a new environment and the opportunity to know her grandfather and cousins.

Once she started her Milestone Map planning, though, Liz was surprised to discover how hard it would be to make the break. She hadn't thought about the part of her heart she'd miss when she left Tulsa behind: her best friends of a dozen years, Marian and Jill. While Liz was certain moving was the right thing to do, she also recognized that her heart would need more gentle handling to make sense of her conflicting emotions. The next image shows a portion of her milestone map ideas.

Let your mind step back to get a sense of the big picture here. You can refer to your roadmap list on a regular basis and take the opportunity to appreciate your progress. The milestones list also reminds you of where you are and what's next for you in this moving journey. You'll find this approach of creating "the big picture" helps you better appreciate the fullness of your change.

Another activity you can add to the Milestone Map is to mark your progress and relocation movement in terms of numbers. For example, would you say that you are about 10 percent through the relocation process? Or 40 percent? Or 75 percent? Once you think you've passed the midway point, then mark that milestone in a special way—an evening out, a day at a spa, a new piece of furniture or accessory for the new house, DVD night, or midday coffee with a friend. Find fun ways to celebrate.

What are your moving milestones?

____

____

____

Your Milestone Map will help you see the big picture of your move. Consider ideas about how you could create that image. Jot down your thoughts here.

____

____

____

Hello Santa Barbara

"Welcome, Liz + Tina!"

Drive 1,500 miles!

Bring camera and journal on the road

Finalize move-in plan, dates, storage

Arrange to frame the photo of Tulsa home

Give notice at work

Have "Memory Lane Lunch" with Jill and Marian

HALFWAY MILESTONE! CELEBRATE!

Contact organizer

Contact real estate agent in Santa Barbara

Schedule Book Club at my house

Browse online for neighborhoods where I want to live

Buy *Santa Barbara: Literary Landscapes* by Peter Treadwell

Tell family and friends we're moving closer to Dad

Begin Santa Barbara area job search

Goodbye Tulsa

Assess your progress in numbers. What percentage of your relocation have you completed?

____

____

____

____

How might you mark and celebrate the midway point in your relocation?

____

____

____

____

Tips That Respect Your Muddled Middle Heart-Stage

What else might you do to guide yourself through this confusing middle stage and bring more clarity into the picture? Here are a few important tips and heart questions to consider.

Tip #1: Walk down memory lane.

In an earlier chapter, you jotted down thoughts about your moving history. Let's walk down memory lane again, this time with the move you experienced before the one you are going through now. What are some of your favorite experiences that you brought from that previous place?

For example, I listed a few of my favorite pastimes before making my recent move. My list included Olive Garden for dinner, gourmet food demonstrations, Starbucks special treat once a week, journal writing outside in the springtime, and enjoying the views at sunset. These are all enjoyable activities that I've continued even after relocating. You can take time to anticipate doing delightful activities like these in your next location, too. They're more important than you might realize.

List favorite pastimes that you've brought into your current life. What activities would you like to bring forth into the new life after your new move?

Tip #2: Plan ahead toward making a special stop en route to your new home.

Here's a tip for those of you who are driving to another state with your move. Go online to MapQuest (www.mapquest.com) or Google Maps (www.maps.google.com) to plot the course from the home you're leaving to the home you're moving to. Go beyond plotting just the main routes you'd like to take for your journey. In addition to visiting Aunt Millie along the way to your new community, add a stop to check out a new special place or perhaps rediscover an old favorite destination you have not seen for many years.

Explore tourist attractions, state parks, or museums. Plan ahead for this extra stop so you're sure of the hours, location, and visitor recommendations. Be sure to pick up one souvenir as a reminder of the journey from here to there.

Also, just for fun, locate a few favorite eateries along the trip. When I was young, my family drove from Indiana to Oklahoma each summer to visit my grandmother. Since this was way before the time of satellite navigational systems and online mapping options, all we could do was to keep an eye out for the billboards on the highway to discover what was coming up the road for a meal stop. As a family, we collectively had one special trip quest: find the next Dairy Queen!

List several ideas for extra special stops en route to your new community.

Tip #3: Express your heart, muddled emotions and all.
It is difficult to work through the emotions that come with the Muddled Middle heart-stage if you haven't given yourself the opportunity to sort through them. Somewhere in that confusing mix, there are both positive and negative feelings.

To get from Muddled to Mindful, you need a means of separating and identifying these conflicting emotions. If you had the opportunity to express, in whatever creative manner you chose, the opposing emotions you're feeling all at once, how would you do that?

Perhaps, like Shannon, you think visually. Shannon developed a large black-and-white photograph of her old home and cut it into segments, rearranged it into a heart-shaped collage, and mounted that heart on an area map of her new home. Her artwork expressed a fear that her concept of "home" would be shattered, yet it also captured Shannon's hope that her "heart" would remain intact no matter where she landed.

Take the opportunity to explore your own confused emotions as well as your creative side now.

What creative outlets do you enjoy? Playing a musical instrument, painting, developing dessert recipes, writing poetry, or taking photographs are just a few examples. Jot down a few ideas about how you can use creative means to express what you're feeling in this heart-stage.

____

____

____

____

____

____

____

Tip #4: Revisit your moving intention question.

In chapter 3, exercise 4, you were invited to create a Heart-of-Your-Move intention question. Revisit that intention query now and reread the answer you wrote down. Does that response still support, guide, and resonate with you during this heart-stage of your relocation journey? If it no longer seems the best fit for you, take a moment now to write a new intention.

Why do this? Because you're putting into action a powerful resource for living your life with purpose. Follow the path of what you intend to create in your new world. If the original intention changes, you may want to walk a new path. Here's a chance to revisit and clarify.

Review your moving intention statement. Does it still inspire and guide you? Write down your responses here.

Chapter Wrap-Up

Be patient with yourself during this Muddled Middle phase. Encourage your creative side to play, laugh, try out new things, explore other approaches, and discover your talents. Let yourself assess the things that may be overdue for a bit of changing. Be as imaginative, inspired, artistic, and inventive as you want to be. Turn muddle into a clearer mindfulness as you stay close to your moving intention.

Take a pause from the craziness of your relocation and spend some time with the *heart* of your move. The upcoming questions are designed to help you gain more understanding and listen to your heart. Then the next chapter—Harmonious Hellos—offers new ways to say hello to your new home and your joyous new life.

Heart Notes to Remember

- The middle phase of the heart of your move is a confusing and perplexing in-between stage. It's the time when you haven't yet let go of the "old you" and you haven't yet embraced the "new you."
- Understand that confusion is a natural by-product of change.
- The source of confusion may come from experiencing a major shift in relationships, location, lifestyle, work environment, culture, climate, or type of community.
- Look for and identify personal anchors. What important people and aspects of your life are not changing?
- Become well informed about your new area. If possible, visit the location before the move.
- Identify one more special change that helps you let go of something that is no longer a good fit for you.
- Step back and get a sense of the big picture of your move. Celebrate at least one milestone.

Reflections for Muddled Middle

By filling a blank page with words, I get to know myself and what I keep locked away in the recesses of my heart and mind.[14]

– Lesléa Newman, *Write from the Heart*

The questions that follow focus on the Muddled Middle heart-stage of the heart of your move. Take a moment to scan the information. Pick at least one question that touches you the most. Write your thoughts and insights here or in your journal. If time permits, respond to more questions offered here.

♥ Anchors are things in your life that help ground you and give you a sense of feeling on an even keel. Identify several anchors that are with you now that can smooth the waves of change.

♥ How can those anchors you identified help you during this move?

- How can you become more informed about your new community? What would you like to learn? How can you find out?

- Is there one small area, drawer, box, or part of your closet that needs a little clearing, cleaning, and organizing? What tiny corner of your life can you bring some order to?

- Perhaps it's time to make one more change. Is there something that doesn't serve you well or has not served you well in the past? Now may be the perfect time to revisit and rethink something that hasn't been working for you in a while. Describe your situation. Identify options that would set up one more change that would benefit you.

Self-Care Strategies for Muddled Middle

Stop for a moment.

Take a relaxing deep breath, then release that breath gradually. Take several more slow, full breaths. Focus on the relaxing effect deep breathing has on your mind and body.

This deep breathing exercise is a simple example of self-care, a way to take a brief but invaluable break from the craziness and chaos of your move.

Be kind to yourself. Devote time to regularly easing the confusion and stress that come with relocation. Look over the questions below and select the ones that best connect with you now.

- *What step, regardless of how small, can you take to reduce and soothe some of the relocation stress right now?*

  ___

  ___

  ___

  ___

- *Take time over a few days to identify an action that demonstrates taking care of you. What might you do to respect and strengthen your mental, physical, or spiritual health during this stage of your moving journey?*

  ___

  ___

  ___

  ___

- Imagine your inner moving mentor as calm and relaxed during this confusing Muddled Middle heart-stage. She has some words of wisdom to share with you about your confusion. What does she say?

- Additional notes about this Muddled Middle heart-stage

9

Harmonious Hellos Heart-Stage

But I've come to believe that what we want and need most of all is to experience a sense of welcome in our own homes.[1]

– Sara Ban Breathnach, *Simple Abundance*

Welcome to the Harmonious Hellos heart-stage, the final phase of the journey through the heart of your move. The clouds of confusion are dissipating and the view of your transition is getting clearer. You've arrived at your new place. Although you still have much to do, you've faced aspects of endings and confusion with courage. Take a relaxing breath.

Integrating change into your life is like saying hello to and developing a relationship with a new friend. This chapter explores ways to say "Hello, new home!" as well as "Hello, new me!" Again, you'll read how seasoned movers faced change and connected with their new lives. Let's start with a few definitions.[2]

Harmonious Hellos Heart-Stage Definitions

Hello/welcome

- To greet someone in a friendly and respectful manner
- To feel welcomed and to one's liking
- A welcoming place that feels agreeable, favorable, gratifying, satisfying

Cassandra's thoughts: neighborly neighbors

Cassandra described her feeling of being welcomed by neighbors in her new community like getting a hug from a friend. Within a week of arriving in her new home in Asheville, two of her neighbors down the street stopped by—one with chocolate chip cookies and the other with espresso brownies in hand. Yummy.

Annabelle's thoughts: one part warmth, one part optimism

Annabelle defined feeling welcomed as emotional sensations. "Feeling welcomed in my new home was like taking one part 'warmth' and one part 'optimism.' I can finally begin to let many of the stressors from this move melt away."

Describe what "feeling welcomed" means to you.

___

___

___

___

___

Harmonious

- The parts sound good individually as well as collectively, like a pleasant tone or melody
- An agreement of opinions as if to say your head and heart are in alignment
- Living in peace and friendship

Denise's thoughts: harmonious synonyms

Denise, an author who moved to Chicago, headed to her personal library resources to dig deeper into the meaning of the word *harmonious.* She typed out her favorite words that communicated her feelings about this final stage of her move. She chose agreeable, frictionless, gratifying, in agreement, in rapport, neighborly, of one mind, smooth, steady, synergetic.

Describe what "harmonious" means to you at this stage of your move.

Home

- A place where one lives, one's residence
- An environment that offers security and happiness
- A sense of origin, such as the city or state where one lives, was born, or lived a long time
- To the center or heart of something; to feel deeply, as in "Your comments really hit home for me."

Sue's thoughts: functional and beautiful
What makes a house a home for Sue, who retired and moved into a condo in Florida? "I'm relaxed. Feel at home. Feel settled. The place is set up in a functional way and an aesthetically beautiful and appealing way. I take pleasure in knowing that I created the room spaces. I know that some rooms will take longer than others to be finished, but the most important rooms are done and ready to enjoy."

Sue also set up a small outdoor balcony space to sit, relax, and enjoy the view of the ocean. "At sunset, we gather near the beach with other residents to toast the setting sun. New friends are on the horizon for me."

What makes a house a home for you?

The Art and Heart—Connecting or Colliding?

This book opened with the idea that we can view a relocation with two different perspectives—the *art* of your move, which includes zillions of details and decisions needed to make a move happen, and the *heart* of your move, which respects the human side of your relocation. In reality, these two perspectives can connect, combine, and sometimes collide throughout the relocation journey.

Colliding is when the head and the heart are at odds about any aspect of the relocation. Your head may say it's a great decision to move and that it fits perfectly with your career path. And your heart may feel quite sad about some of the losses happening with the move. If you've acknowledged and attended to both aspects of the move all along, chances are your Hellos will be more harmonious.

Women experience diverse thoughts which may be confusing—especially in the Harmonious Hello heart-stage. Remember that "confusion" is a common by-product of change. Please do not consider this conflict of head and heart as "bad." It is quite natural to have opposing thoughts. Working through them can be helpful in acknowledging and clarifying your true feelings. Also, remember that you are never alone in feeling the way you do.

Here is an example of the art and heart in conflict:

ART of Moving *This is a smart decision. The new job will offer solid working experience. And there are many opportunities for advancement.*

HEART of Moving *I've lived here in this home for eleven years. My best friends and my sister live here. Sometimes I feel such sadness about leaving.*

But the art and heart can also connect, cooperate, and be in sync:

ART of Moving *I'm organized and I labeled things well when we packed.*

HEART of Moving *I'm so glad and grateful that I spent the extra time to organize, label, and keep track of all my items in our boxes. The unpacking went more quickly and smoothly, and was more relaxing for me with this move.*

Being well organized in your initial packing will help the eventual unpacking go faster and more smoothly. I remember both the good and the bad with my move from the Midwest to the Southwest. I prided myself on being an exceptionally well-organized packer—for about 90 percent of the boxes. The last 10 percent, though, contained items from all over the pre-move house. Somehow, I also lost the list of the items for those boxes.

Although I can laugh about it now, at the time I just shook my head in frustration when I opened one of these unorganized containers. To encourage a bit of coping then, I just set a timer for an hour and forged through the task as a special project. I allowed myself the choice of renewing a second hour if needed, or refocusing on other, more joyful tasks.

Remember, it's important that both *art* and *heart* are well attended to during your relocation journey. As a result, you'll experience more Harmonious Hellos after the move.

Are the art and heart of your relocation colliding or connecting? Share an example of each. Feel free to adapt this exercise to match your ideas.

COLLIDING Art and Heart Thoughts

Art of Moving thoughts

____

____

____

Heart of Moving thoughts

____

____

____

CONNECTING Art and Heart Thoughts

Art of Moving thoughts

____

____

____

Heart of Moving thoughts

____

____

____

Feeling Unsettled When You Expect to Feel Settled

Many women feel *un*settled after making a move. After all, we're usually the ones who keep the ball rolling with the *art* of our moves by unpacking, arranging furniture, hanging pictures, and so on. Add to that the quest of finding the right doctor, dentist, veterinarian, babysitter, decorator, bank, handyman, and more. We are keenly aware that the pieces are indeed falling into place. Yet, during your Harmonious Hellos heart-stage, you still may feel discomfort, conflicting emotions, and stress, as the following women commented.

Rita: thinking, thinking, thinking

Rita shared a few ups and downs with her move. "We moved from a noisy neighborhood to a larger home in a quiet subdivision across town, so I didn't anticipate any problems after the move. In the new calm, I was surprised to find moving still wasn't exactly stress-free. The hardest part of the unpacking phase was that everything required thought. The flurry of activity required me to be focused, deliberate, and mindful. I recall being very tired at the end of each day."

Maria: not an oddball

"I thought I'd be just fine after the move," Maria told me. "Instead, it felt like I was wearing clothes that just didn't fit. It was so odd. Now I know that other women can feel this way. I'm not such an oddball after all."

Joan: feeling disoriented

Joan said she "felt strange and disoriented" after her move. "For many years we lived in the same house. Before I moved, I knew where everything was. Now I'm lucky to find the toothbrush and toothpaste, much less my bras!" (Note: Joan eventually found her bras.)

Have you recently moved? If you feel somewhat unsettled, describe those feelings here.

Making Harmonious Connections

Experiencing your Harmonious Hellos heart-stage is much more than moving into your new place. You're empowered to create a whole host of new connections. And each connection says something about you and what is important to you.

To feel at home in your own heart, be mindful, patient, and understanding. Remember, the *heart* of your move clock ticks slower than the unpacking clock. Projects that will take more time may include

- Setting up a business or feeling comfortable in a new job.
- Getting to know the neighbors and the neighborhood.
- Becoming familiar with family members' new connections (partner's work or children's school).
- Nurturing new friendships.
- Learning firsthand about your community.
- Becoming involved in personal or spiritual interests like worship activities, clubs, programs, or supporting causes.
- Learning new ways to connect and keep in touch with the friends or family you left behind in your previous hometown.

Yes, you're going through a transition that continues long after the move. In effect, you are aligning, realigning, and creating the new *you* as you make choices that reflect the connections that are valuable to you. Here are a few examples of how women enhanced their post-move connections:

Marian: connecting with the great outdoors

Marian and her husband are avid outdoor people who enjoy hiking. After retirement, they selected Colorado Springs for their home community and found a home with hiking trailheads right across the street from their front lawn.

Barbara: book club and writing classes

Barbara's fondness for good mystery books led her to the Barnes & Noble mystery book club, which met once a month. One of the members of the club had a daughter the same age as Barbara's daughter. Both the mothers and the daughters started new friendships. Another club member mentioned an online mystery writing class that Barbara registered for. It nurtured her love of writing and connected her with like-minded people.

My experience: acting class for beginners

After a previous move, I signed up for an acting class through the university adult education program. The students had tons of fun in this class. We were encouraged to stretch ourselves in new directions and get out of our comfort zones. Through this class, I forged fantastic friendships including one friend whom I chose to be my bridesmaid in my wedding.

What valuable connections do you want to establish? List three connections you'd like to forge and jot down any ideas you have to make them happen.

1. ______________________________

____

2. ______________________________

____

3. ______________________________

____

Making New Connections through Volunteering

Get involved. That's one of the most frequently offered suggestions from today's moving resources for connecting with your new community. You can get involved in so many different ways: volunteering, joining a club, and offering to serve or lead committees and organizations.

Community outreach efforts result in feel-good moments and heart-touching experiences. My husband, Scott, and I support an outreach program through our church called the Sandwich Squad. Every six weeks, Scott and I prepare twenty-four sack lunches. Other Early Bird members from the 7:30 a.m. service prepare lunches the same way. Then these meals—a total of 100 to 150 lunches each time—are delivered to the community organization that distributes them to a local women and children's crisis shelter.

My husband and I also create "blessing bags," which are bags of snacks, basic toiletries, and where-to-find-help literature for the homeless people we encounter in our city. We keep these bags in each of our cars so we're able to give one away to someone in need as we come and go. In each blessing bag, I also include a copy of favorite inspirational quotations and poems.

Patty: connections with a cause

Patty's desired connections honored her affection for animals. "I grew up on a farm and love animals. I'm committed to supporting animal rescue causes. One of the first connections I made after my move was to find and visit the local Humane Society and greyhound rescue group to explore volunteer opportunities. My dog Maxwell, a retired greyhound, is my buddy. He helped me through the stress of this last move."

Heather: meeting, joining, networking

Heather, an event planner who recently moved to New York City, joined the local chapter of a women's networking association.

After the second luncheon meeting, she signed up to be on the annual holiday auction committee that met each month for six months leading up to the event.

Heather walked into a true win-win situation. Her committee was thrilled to have her and the event planner experience she brought on board. And Heather was excited about networking with local businesswomen and making great contacts to help build her business. Their efforts produced a fun and highly successful holiday affair.

Eva: teaching her children to make a difference

Eva and her family were settled in their new home only a few months when Eva read about the Make a Difference Day national event sponsored by *USA Weekend*.[3] She knew she wanted to instill in her young children the spirit of giving. Here was the perfect opportunity.

A nearby assisted living facility inspired their efforts. Eva called the activities director and asked for ideas that would be appreciated by any of the residents. The director said that three residents had birthdays in the upcoming month and would enjoy having handmade birthday cards.

Eva and her children were invited to the center to meet the three ladies, sing a birthday song, and hand them each a card. Eva also brought along balloons and a single rose for each birthday gal. Based on the smiles alone, Eva wasn't sure who enjoyed the experience the most—the three honored residents or her two children.

Karen Duncan, the coauthor of *The Good Fun! Book: 12 Months of Parties That Celebrate Service*,[4] introduced her children to volunteering when they were young. As they grew older, she and her husband, Arne (who became U.S secretary of education in 2009), encouraged them to be more self-directed in their helping activities. "Kids who help others help themselves, too. Studies show that students who volunteer tend to do better in school and are less likely to engage in risky behaviors."[5]

Do you see the common thread? All strong connections that benefit others will benefit ourselves in positive ways.

Heart ♥ Memo

Making Friends while Going Green

After moving her family, Mindy was quite surprised to discover that her new neighborhood did not offer weekly curbside recycling. Losing access to this convenient service encouraged Mindy to rethink her magazine subscriptions. She had already switched her printed professional journals to online versions, and now it was time to consider what other magazines she could let go of or enjoy as apps on her electronic tablet. She said goodbye to several of her print magazines and said hello to a lifestyle magazine app that featured her new city.

A quick online search also yielded recycling center information, locations, and maps. She used some of her moving boxes to create her home recycling center. Once the boxes were nearly full, she scheduled a time to drop off her things. Mindy also identified new shopping areas and restaurants located along the way so she could pair up her recycling efforts with the exploration of her new city.

One day as Mindy was loading up her hybrid SUV for a trip to the recycling center, her neighbor Sonya waved hello from her mailbox. The two struck up a conversation. Mindy had been contemplating a school project her son Jake was working on for the upcoming Earth Day and "A Billion Acts of Green" movement.[6] Mother and son had brainstormed about simple ways to reduce, reuse, and recycle. Mindy asked Sonya if she'd like to join their team to help organize several neighborhood activities.

Their team effort led to a paper drive, the planting of ten new trees on their block, and the creation of a "going green" ideas ebooklet, which included a link to a footprint calculator. Both mom and son forged new friendships in the process.

Consider one small gesture of volunteering you might explore as you connect with your new community. For those of you moving with children, include ideas for them, too. Jot down your thoughts here.

Building a New Nest that Reflects You

As you unpack, you make many choices about how to set up your home and where you'd like to put things. Many women find this process of "building a nest" satisfying, exhilarating, exciting, joyful, and confidence-building—words that reflect the heart of a move. Why? Because they're making decisions that harmonize with their tastes, preferences, and values.

Tessa: in charge of her own place

"Moving into my new apartment was exhilarating," Tessa said after her recent divorce. "I'm in charge of this new place and can decorate however I want. I love sunflowers, so every room has a sunflower item in it."

Carole: bringing in her favorite color

Carole used a similar strategy when she moved into her new apartment in Houston after graduating from Purdue University. Because she was fond of the color blue, she put something blue in every room.

Renee: creating a library nook

With her retirement a few years away, Renee decided to sell her home and rent a temporary place to live. She downsized from her four-bedroom house to a rented two-bedroom town house.

Her landlord agreed that the place needed some TLC and updating. He gave her permission to fix up and decorate the town house as long as she was comfortable signing a one-year lease. He provided the paint and paid for a couple of the upgrades.

Despite the smaller quarters, Renee loved her new place. A coat of pastel green paint softened the stark white walls and complemented her furniture. A window bench seat was recovered with flowered fabric. A garden theme emerged. She removed the door of the nearby closet and tucked in a bookcase. Soon she had created her own little library nook with the window bench area nearby to read and relax.

Renee not only set up her home, but she also secured a special place that gave her a sense of retreat and sanctuary.

Dana: new outdoor space with relaxing view

Due to health changes, Dana and her husband, David, had to move from a third-floor condo with beautiful vaulted ceilings to a first-floor condo that seemed cave-like by comparison.

Although they lost the expansive ceilings, they were thrilled that their first-floor condo included a patio with a great view of the courtyard fountain beyond. The couple brightened this patio by purchasing planters with colorful flowers, several bird feeders, and new patio furniture. By bringing the outside in, their efforts made the whole condo much more relaxing and enjoyable.

How might you look at your space in a new way and make it more colorful and functional for your tastes and hobbies? List your ideas here.

Explore the Spirit of Intention with Feng Shui

Shortly after my move to Tucson, I visited a local bookstore. Browsing the home decorating section, I discovered books on feng shui. Feng shui, whose origins are linked with ancient Chinese principles, is now applied to home placement, organization, and design that promote a greater sense of intention.

One of my favorite books on this topic is *Living Feng Shui: Personal Stories* by Carole J. Hyder, an author I met at a local book signing. I love how reader-friendly and engaging this book is. "One of the basic principles of feng shui is that your space mirrors your life," Carol shared in her book's introduction. "It follows that you will get a new perspective on your life by using feng shui tools. They can provide ways to create a space that will bring about prosperity, productivity, partners, and peace."[7]

I became fascinated by the decorating, arranging, placement, and clearing-the-clutter aspects of feng shui and soon gathered quite a collection of related books—including those by author Terah Kathryn Collins. Applying an intentional mindset, I used many of the principles when I created the floor plans for each of our rooms. For example, one feng shui principle for furnishing an office is not to have your back to the doorway.[8] So in my home office, I placed the main computer desk where I had a comfortable view of the door and placed attractive lamps on the desk to light my workspace.

Jenny: transforming her home

Shortly after her move to Minnesota, Jenny attended a women's networking meeting and met Elaina, a feng shui consultant. Jenny invited Elaina over to her new home. Elaina offered several suggestions for how the rooms might flow easily as well as ways to bring more light into dark areas of the house and offered tips (called cures) for one problem area.

Jenny was so intrigued with feng shui that the next time she took her young son to story time at their local bookstore, she browsed through the decorating section. There, she found a large selection of feng shui resources and picked out several to purchase. She soon became a student of feng shui by collecting, reading, and applying ideas from her new books to her own home.

Clearing the clutter is a major theme in feng shui. This holds to the idea that energy (called chi) should flow easily through each room. Jenny wanted to get a handle on the clutter in her son's room, which boasted a large picture window but a tiny closet. Her husband, who doubled as a handyman over the weekend, helped her construct new built-in shelves wrapped around the picture window. The shelves included drawers and cabinetry with doors for extra toy storage. Jenny's husband also added a long bench at the base of the window, which provided a great space for home story time.

Placing items in your home with the spirit of intention can reaffirm what is important to you and what you want to emphasize in your new life.

Reestablish a Favorite Tradition

One of my favorite Heart of Moving strategies is to schedule special recurring events and activities after your move. You can reestablish a tradition from your previous home that was near and dear to your heart or create new traditions that nurture your spirit.

After we moved from Missouri to Arizona, my husband Scott and I spent a portion of our unpacking time setting up our TV room because we looking forward to reestablishing a favorite tradition: theme evenings.

Tuesday evening is usually reserved as our travel theme night. When we planned our once-in-a-lifetime trip to Egypt, we spent our Tuesday evenings watching the Teaching Company DVD lessons taught by Professor Bob Brier or the Discovery Channel and PBS documentaries on the pharaohs and the pyramids.[9] When we planned our trip to California, we watched documentaries that featured Yosemite National Park and interesting places to visit like the Monterey Bay Aquarium.

Our Saturday evenings are usually devoted to historical period British mysteries, and we draw upon our large collection of Agatha Christie-inspired shows. That tradition includes taking a break in the middle of the show to make a delicious batch of popcorn.

Jasmine: Monday mornings at the eat-in bakery
Before her move, Jasmine and her husband Jay usually started their Monday mornings at an eat-in bakery located just across from the university where they worked. Each Monday, Jay would try out different pastries while Jasmine faithfully ordered her delicious banana nut muffin. For them, this tradition represented a special way to start their work week.

Once they arrived in their new city, Jasmine looked around and discovered another small eat-in bakery located fairly close to their new home. She and Jay reestablished their Monday morning tradition, but she admitted to a small tweak in her ritual. She switched her allegiance to a scrumptious zucchini nut muffin.

What favorite traditions do you want to reinstate at your new place or community? List them here.

____

____

____

____

Develop New Rituals

In addition to reestablishing an old tradition, why not create a new one?

Alexandra Stoddard defines rituals as "patterns you create in your everyday living that uplift the way you do ordinary things." In her book *Living a Beautiful Life*, Alexandra has filled each chapter with great suggestions for creating new rituals. The author closed her chapters with Grace Notes—a collection of simple ways to add joy, beauty, and order to your home.[10] I so much enjoy Alexandra's books and always find great inspiration for new favorite rituals.

After Meg Cox became a mother in 1994, she started her quest to find contemporary rituals that would enhance her family's traditions. She used her career skills as a journalist to interview diverse families. She wanted to discover unique, interesting, and fun ways families celebrate special days and events. "I like to say that family ritual is pretty much anything families do together deliberately, as long as it's juiced up with some flourish that lifts it above the humdrum routine," Meg explains in *The Book of New Family Traditions: How to Create Great Rituals for Holidays and Every Day.*[11]

Although this book is geared primarily toward families, I found lots of great, creative, fun, and funny ideas for those who have children or not. It gives you a chance to tap into your inner creative kid by letting its ideas inspire new ideas that you can adapt to your own situation.

For example, I love the delightful and endearing birthday ritual suggestion in her book about a mother who lined the staircase to the second floor on both sides with stuffed animals.[12] At the top of the staircase, the mother placed her son's first present for his birthday. That idea inspired my Valentine's Day adaptation of placing paper cut-out hearts along the sides of the only steps we have, which happen to go into the house from the garage. Then the box at the top step provided a clue for my husband as to the location of his hidden Valentine's Day gift.

Michelle: new traditions for newlyweds

Newlyweds Michelle and Mark moved into their new place and quickly started up several new rituals, the first of which was to welcome each weekend together with the clink of wine glasses, a toast, and relaxing tunes to complement their meals. For example, they've chosen the melodies of Italian music to accompany pasta dishes.

On the first Friday of the month, Mark picks up flowers for his sweetheart on his way home from work and Michelle prepares a "winner" meal. Every other month, they try out new recipes and add their most delicious meals to their winners' circle. Since both of them love to cook, they alternate who's the chef and who's the assistant chef.

List the new traditions and rituals you'd like to start in your new environment or ways to get creative with a new routine.

Celebrate Memorable Holidays

Did you know that March 26 is Make Up Your Own Holiday Day?[13]

You don't have to be the president of the United States to declare special holidays—like when President Ronald Reagan proclaimed the third Sunday in July to be National Ice Cream Day.[14] So (drumroll please), I decree the 1st of May to officially be The Heart of Your Move Day!

Think about some of your favorite or even silly things you enjoy. For example, if you're a serious fan of chocolate like I am, then you might create a Sinful Chocolate Desserts Day. By the way, for you chocolate lovers, there are about fifteen different national chocolate days listed on one online website. October 28 is the official National Chocolate Day.[15]

Another fun holiday you can enjoy is She's Funny That Way Day.[16] This special day on March 31 honors the funny ladies we are fortunate to remember or have in our lives. Which women make you smile and tickle your funny bone? What antics of theirs are so funny?

For parents and teachers, check out *The Teacher's Calendar: The Day-by-Day Almanac of Historic Events, Holidays, Famous Birthdays and More!*[17] It's filled with innovative ideas for lessons, bulletin boards, reports, and calendars. This resource includes historical anniversaries, birthdays, biographies, astronomical phenomena, holidays from all major religions and nations, famous firsts, and scientific and space milestones.

If a day isn't enough to embrace the fullness of your new holiday, then how about naming a whole month? Create your own or jump on the bandwagon of unique months already set on the calendar. You could even embrace one of the notable months starting three, four, or five months after your move with your own renditions of how to celebrate. *Chase's Calendar of Events* provides an extensive list to explore.[18] Some of my favorites include: Get Organized Month (January), National Humor Month (April), What Will Be Your Legacy Month (August), International Women's Friendship Month (September), and Adopt-a-Shelter-Dog Month (October).

Cassie: a day that honors her favorite winter location

You can also look at your relocation for inspiration. Cassie created her own "I Miss the Snow" holiday after she moved to the desert. On that day, she surfs the Internet for beautiful snow-drenched photos and revisits her own photos from the Utah slopes. She calls her best friend from her previous snowy city and together they plan ahead some trips for the upcoming winter. During these return visits, she and her friend travel to the slopes, make a snowman at the house, and enjoy a friendly snowball fight.

What special holiday would you like to create and why? How would you like to celebrate that day?

Heart ♥ Memo

National Moving Month

Did you know that May is National Moving Month? The American Moving and Storage Association selected May as the busy time on the calendar when most people start relocating themselves and their stuff. Although people move throughout the year, the relocation industry considers May through September to be the moving season. Approximately thirty-five million Americans move each year.[19]

Tips for Enhancing Your Harmonious Hellos

How does the Harmonious Hellos stage compare to the other two stages? Connecting with new things (saying hello) may flow more easily than the tough disconnecting part (saying goodbye) and the muddled middle stage. Still, we are unique women with unique situations, personalities, and histories. Consider these five additional tips for enriching your Harmonious Hellos part of the relocation.

Tip #1: Be a tourist in your new community.

After my parents moved our family to Independence, Missouri, on the outskirts of Kansas City, my father decided we needed to become tourists in our new community. Dad loved history, so on one of our first weekend outings, we visited the Truman Library and Museum, which recounts the life of Harry S. Truman, our nation's thirty-third president. What a surprise to find out that people who'd lived in the area for years had never taken the time to visit this site.

To be a tourist in your own town, search online to learn about some of the key sites in and around your new city. Then visit the sites after you've arrived.

Jot down one or two places you could visit as a tourist in or near your new community.

___

___

___

___

Tip #2: Host your own welcome party.

After your move, why not host a welcome party for yourself and your family? In her book *Moving with Kids: 25 Ways to Ease Your Family's Transition to a New Home,* Lori Collins Burgan wrote that having a party is especially fun when you involve your kids in the planning.[20] Making invitations and helping the kids deliver them door to door opens up lots of opportunities to make new friends in your neighborhood.

For the summertime, Lori suggested hosting an ice cream sundae party on the driveway. For the wintertime in locations that enjoy lots of snow, consider having a sledding party followed by hot chocolate and cookies.

Lori's book is filled with lots of ideas for parents to help their children with the transition of moving. It's at the top of my favorite books that honor the heart of moving. (You'll also find a great list of relocation books for children in the "Books for Parents and Kids" section coming up in part IV.)

Lucy: welcome to my family party

Lucy believed that her family's arrival at their new home in Nashville completed a major goal and milestone. Without waiting until every box was unpacked, she invited the neighbors over and hosted her own "Welcome to My Family" party. Their young son Matt handed out name tags. Her husband, Ron, served up hot dogs on his new grill. Their teenage daughter Kelly played the role of home reporter and took lots of photographs with her digital camera. Lucy supervised the joyful, fun celebration.

Jot down your own welcome party ideas.

____

____

____

Tip #3: Release at least one self-imposed rule.

From time to time, I surprise myself when I realize I'm holding onto an old self-imposed rule that could—and should—be released.

After my move to Arizona, I remember visiting a local bookstore and browsing through the audio books. For some unknown reason, I had this self-imposed rule that said, "Carolyn, you are to listen to only one audio book at a time." The addendum to that rule said, "You will select only nonfiction audio books that promote ways to enhance your business." I know, it does sound silly. Well, I quickly released that rule and now enjoy listening to both fiction and nonfiction in the car and on my exercise bicycle. In effect, moving gave me permission to make a change that opened up a whole new world of bestselling fiction, thrillers, and mysteries.

As you experience the Harmonious Hellos heart-stage of your move, assess and reassess your self-imposed rules. See which ones you can modify or say goodbye to. Look at ways to be more flexible and more open to changes that better fit you.

What is one self-imposed rule that you can release or modify?

____

____

____

Tip #4: Try out something that's unlike the usual you.

Now is the time to explore new sides of yourself. Consider trying out some things that the usual *you* wouldn't normally do.

If you're not a talkative kind of gal, then encourage yourself to engage in conversation with new people you meet. If you're usually a talkative kind of person, give yourself relaxing quiet time to look around and observe your new surroundings.

If you're someone who rarely dresses up, then you might do a makeover day followed by a special dinner out. Or if you always dress to the nines, then let yourself have a casual day. One time I encouraged myself to try on clothes with colors that were "not me." I tend to not wear bold colors, so I gave myself a just-for-fun assignment of trying on bright green, bright orange, and bright yellow the next time I shopped the sales.

Here's another example: Eliza always headed to the business section of books at the bookstore. One day, although she did not have a green thumb, she decided to head to the gardening section to browse the books on that topic.

Think about the "as usual" you and explore ways to safely change things up and have fun with it!

Heart ♥ Memo

Expanding Your Comfort Zone

Stepping out of your comfort zone can also produce positive results in the friend-finding department. Rachel Bertsche, the author of *MWF Seeking BFF*, went on a yearlong quest to find new best friends after her move to Chicago. She broke the "as usual" mold by letting herself act silly at Second City's improv class and dancing a flash mob routine on a cold rainy street. "Relationships are solidified in these vulnerable, step-outside-the-box, how-did-I-get-here moments," writes Rachel.[21]

♡ *What ideas might you try out that are unlike the usual you?*

____

____

____

Tip #5: Soften the hard deadlines.

Do you have any self-imposed deadlines you might be able to flex a bit?

In the flurry of unpacking and taking care of the art of your move, why not identify chores or activities that you can handle later? For example, Trudy had originally set up certain post-moving goals that gave her a deadline of one month to set up her home office and hire a personal assistant. When her settling-in time took longer than expected, she softened her deadline to give herself three to six months. It also softened her stress.

Of course, some deadlines are precise and have no wiggle room. If your moving van is arriving on a particular day, then it's best to be there prepared to meet the movers. However, other deadlines may be more easily softened. As you set up your schedules, give yourself time extensions whenever you can.

I used to have a strict deadline of January 1 to review the goals for the previous year that just wrapped up *and* create the goals for the new upcoming year. Not surprisingly, I found this deadline added even more stress to a busy December holiday season. Now I've softened that deadline and allow myself to work on reviews and goal setting during the whole month of January. I'm glad and relieved that I extended my planning project to after the holidays when it's less hectic for me.

What upcoming deadlines might be softened? List them here.

____

____

____

____

Chapter Wrap-Up

Marking the arrival into your Harmonious Hello heart-stage honors the long, emotional journey that started with saying goodbye and continued with traveling through the clouds of confusion. When sojourning through this last stage of the move, the path usually starts to feel easier—like a fog has been lifted so you can see more clearly.

Setting up your "home sweet home" can be both exhilarating and exhausting. You are actually saying Harmonious Hellos to your new home, your new community, and most important, to the new *you* that's evolving. In the midst of the activity, always be sure to create a space where your spirit feels safe, nurtured, and inspired.

Heart Notes to Remember

- The Harmonious Hellos heart-stage is the third and final phase of the heart-of-your-move journey.
- Even after you unpack your boxes and arrange your furniture, you may still feel unsettled. Be patient with yourself. It's normal to have those feelings.
- Don't forget, the heart-of-your-move timetable runs slower than the actual move. It may even take up to five years to feel fully comfortable and settled.
- You accomplish saying hello to your new home and new life by the many choices that reflect you, who you are, and the new lifestyle you wish to create.
- Help soothe the stress by creating at least one special spot in your home where you can relax and restore your spirit.
- After your move, explore ways to offer the gift of giving to yourself and to others.

Reflections for Harmonious Hellos

We should write because writing is good for the soul.[22]

Julia Cameron, *The Right to Write*

Unpacking your belongings and connecting with your new home may signal the end of your relocation work, but not your heart work. There is still the underlying journey of feeling at home and feeling truly settled in.

To help you reflect more deeply about the Harmonious Hellos heart-stage, pick one question below that touches you the most, then write your thoughts and insights here or in your journal. You may also want to consider the other questions and glean even more insights into your own feelings.

♥ Describe the vision you have for your new home. Write down what your heart would love to feel as you set up your new nest.

____

____

____

____

____

____

____

____

____

- How might you create a special place in your new home that encourages a feeling of a retreat or sanctuary?

- Take some time to think about the rituals and traditions you have in your life. Express what it is about them that helps you feel anchored.

- Share one or two new interests you would like to cultivate after the move. What might you do to learn more?

- Describe any challenges you may have during this time of your move. How might you face those challenges in ways that show personal support and encouragement?

- Give yourself a thank you gift for facing the heart of your move with courage and resolve. Jot down your gift ideas here.

Self-Care Strategies for Harmonious Hellos

You may be surprised when unexpected stress, confusion, and frustration—even feelings of loss—pop up during the Harmonious Hello heart-stage. After all, it's a time when you expect things to fall into place.

I suggest you review the heart questions below and select at least one question to answer here or in your journal. Take time to seek out and find strategies that support you at this time.

♥ *What single step—regardless of how small—can you take to reduce and soothe some of the stress you're feeling during this stage of your move?*

____

____

____

____

____

____

♥ *Identify an action that demonstrates taking great care of yourself. What might you do to respect and strengthen your mental, physical, or spiritual health during the Harmonious Hellos heart-stage?*

____

____

____

____

____

____

♥ Your inner moving mentor is calm and relaxed. She has words of wisdom to share with you about this Harmonious Hellos heart-stage. What does she say?

♥ What other feelings, insights, and ideas may be surfacing that need to be acknowledged or acted upon? Name them here.

♥ What personal listen-to-your-heart questions would you like to ask yourself right now?

My Heartfelt Wishes

The journey through the heart of your move creates
a personal awakening—a private encouragement to look within,
to glimpse upon the evolution of the new you.

– Carolyn Masters

Dear Courageous Reader,

You'll experience so many connections with your move. Thank you for choosing my book as one of those valued connections. Kudos to you for adding new skills that honor the heart of your move and respect the personal side of your relocation.

You've also discovered three heart-focused stages and have gained valuable insights from the experts—women who have survived and thrived through their moves.

- During the *Gracious Goodbyes* heart-stage chapter, you learned that endings are a natural occurrence during a major change. Identifying what you will lose as a result of your move encourages you to explore ways to say your goodbyes with full respect.
- During the *Muddled Middle* heart-stage chapter, you learned that feelings of disorientation and bewilderment are normal

responses to making such a huge transition. Identifying what is not changing gives you something precious to hold onto. Listening to your heart helps you turn the Muddled Middle heart-stage into a Mindful Middle.

- During the *Harmonious Hellos* heart-stage chapter, you learned that getting settled goes beyond simply unpacking boxes and arranging furniture. Reestablishing previous traditions and creating new ones are heartwarming ways to say *hello* to your new home and new you.

Although the three stages in the heart-of-your-move journey were distinct and well separated in this book, please remember that you can experience any or all of the stages before, during, or after your move. And you may not be able to predict ahead of time all the losses that will occur with your move. Some may pop up unexpectedly after the move. For example, after our move to the Southwest, I was surprised how much I missed the smell of freshly mowed grass and the beauty of the Midwest trees in the autumn when they displayed their brilliant art show of changing leaves.

Let your inner moving mentor support you with heartfelt thoughts of confidence. You are a brave and courageous woman. Your evolution continues. A new chapter has opened and you are the author.

Best wishes to you and your move.

Warm regards,

Carolyn

P.S. We've just wrapped up the workbook side of things here, but please don't pack this book just yet. Browse through "Explore New Resources" coming up next in part IV. Many more helpful, heartful ideas are there, waiting for you to make them part of your moving adventure.

Part IV

Explore New Resources

Relocation Books

Here are just a few notes for you regarding your Relocation Books section.

This segment covers three groups of books: Heart of Moving, Art of Moving, and Books for Parents and Kids. You'll find that many books include personal notes from me about the book's content and approach, why I've selected it as one of my favorite choices for that group, as well as its availability. I've also included books that were highly recommended by others or received strong reviews.

And, just for fun, I even created special awards for selected books I felt extra warm-hearted toward. You'll see those in my book notes.

Some books listed here may be out of print, but you may still find new copies through each author's website or used copies through online bookstores.

One last note before you dive into these wonderful books: Several times during the process of writing *The Heart of Your Move,* I happened upon another neat, helpful moving resource that I hadn't seen before. Just as my manuscript was finally ready to go to press, I discovered yet another resource I wished I had been able to include. To remedy my disappointment with not being able to share every one of those exciting discoveries with you, I'm starting a new project: a much more extensive resource guide that will be posted on my book's website, www.TheHeartOfYourMove.com. I look forward to sharing the new, expanded online resource guide later this season.

Heart of Moving Books

Bertsche, Rachel. *MWF Seeking BFF: My Yearlong Search for a New Best Friend*. New York: Ballantine Books, 2011.

After her move to Chicago to be near her fiancé, the author feels her new life is almost complete. What's missing? Best friends in her new city. Join Rachel as she develops and implements a fun and adventurous plan to nurture strong friendships with other women.

Emerson, Margaret, and Catherine Cameron. *Moving: The Challenge of Change*. Nashville: Abingdon Press, 1988.

This book pays high respect to the issues and concerns surrounding the heart of moving. Well researched. Includes many from-the-heart comments from those who have moved. Contains an entire chapter devoted to making the decision to move. Although this book is no longer in print, you may be able to locate copies at Amazon.com.

Goodwin, Cathy. *Making the Big Move: How to Transform Relocation into a Creative Life Transition*. Oakland, CA: New Harbinger Publications, Inc., 1999.

This encouraging book is filled with many examples designed to help you understand the emotional journey and minimize the stress of your move. Each chapter includes quick and easy-to-do exercises that address common situations faced during a move and offers tips for coping with the issues at hand. Examples: Acknowledging aspects of your identity connected with your previous home and work, facing your fears, and integration tips for after the move.

Levine, Leslie. *Will This Place Ever Feel Like Home? Simple Advice for Settling In After You Move*. New York: Contemporary Books (Division of McGraw-Hill Companies), 2002.

One of my favorite books which received my Best Book award featuring the Heart of Your Move. Leslie truly respects that moving can cause frustration and distress. The tone of the author's voice feels calming.

The author covers a multitude of suggestions for facing the details of a relocation with grace. This is an excellent, well-written book to consider even before you move. I'd highly recommend this book to those who are moving and for those who help women going through a relocation.

McCollum, Audrey, Nadia Jensen, and Stuart Copans. *Smart Moves: Your Guide through the Emotional Maze of Relocation*. Manchester, NH: Smith and Kraus Publishers, 1996.

Another book that is devoted to supporting readers as they face emotional stresses of moving. Includes lots of information and exercises that help readers clarify their roles during the move and strengthen their connections with their loved ones. One chapter devoted to moving with a partner shares helpful strategies and exercises to face the move together as well as ways to connect and topics for discussion if the move means some time apart.

Miller, Susan. *After the Boxes Are Unpacked: Moving On After Moving In*. Carol Stream, IL: Tyndale House Publishers, Inc., 1995.

Filled with suggestions for connecting with a new home by viewing the settling-in process through a Christian perspective.

Chapters include a "Heart Talk" that offers an extra dose of support, a "Survival Kit" that suggests a multitude of ways to integrate more peacefulness and coping, and biblical quotations that match Susan's themes.

Art of Moving Books

Allen, Jamie, and Kazz Regelman, eds. *How to Survive a Move: By Hundreds of Happy People Who Did*. Atlanta: Hundreds of Heads Books, Inc., 2005.

I discovered a wealth of *art* and *heart* ideas from this unique book written for both men and women. The editors have collected helpful comments from contributors who have moved before. Just a gentle warning here: different people have different perspectives. Glean your favorites.

Dewkett, Bonnie Joy. *The Joyful Organizer's Guide to a Joyful Move: Everything You Need to Know to Stay Organized During Your Family's Move*. Ridgefield, CT: The Joyful Organizer, LLC, 2011.

A former relocation specialist and professional organizer offers a colorful and organized workbook for keeping track of the details of moving.

Giehl, Nancy, and Joan Hobbs. *Organize Pack Move!: Strategies and Money-Saving Ideas to Simplify Your Move*. Boulder, CO: Simple Moves, 2009.

Here is an excellent, well-organized workbook by the owners of Simple Moves, a company that offers local services to help people organize, pack, and unpack. I like how the authors have sorted the information into five primary sections: preparing, organizing, moving, settling in, checklists. Each of the 75 topics is set up in an easy-to-scan page. The index is an extra bonus that many other workbooks are lacking. Well done.

Kozik, Donna, and Tara Maras. *29 Days to a Smooth Move: Save Your Cents, Save Your Sanity, Save Scads of Your Time*. New York: iUniverse, 2005.

Fun self-published book from two gals who've teamed up to share their ideas on moving. Few moving books have as many humorous stories sprinkled throughout as this one. The book's primary focus is the details associated with moving through suggestions designed to save you time and money. Some of their writing questions ("Make a Moving Memo") and one of the chapters address the emotions of moving.

Poage, Martha. *The Moving Survival Guide: All You Need to Know to Make Your Move Go Smoothly*. Guilford, CT: The Globe Pequot Press, 2005.

Martha's well-organized, insightful book receives my award for Best Art of Moving guide. I've read quite a few books on the details of moving. Written by an executive's wife and a mom who has moved many times, Martha's book is by far the best organized and easy to scan for valuable information if you're facing a busy schedule.

The guide also offers an extraordinarily comprehensive set of moving lists and checklists. Also great for moms and dads looking for ideas to help their kids connect with new schools.

Books for Parents and Kids

Fortunately, there's a wealth of heartwarming resources for children who are moving. I've only scratched the surface. Here's a sampling of my favorites, several books recommended by others, and a few I found on Amazon.com. I've also noted the suggested ages for those resources which provided that information.

Just another quick note: This section provides a list of nonfiction books. As I mentioned before, I'm currently collecting ideas for additional resources, including children's fiction books, to post on our book's website. We're looking forward to expanding this resource listing for kids, parents, teachers, and school counselors.

Burgan, Lori Collins. *Moving With Kids: 25 Ways to Ease Your Family's Transition to a New Home.* Boston: The Harvard Common Press, 2007.

This extraordinary book received my award for Best Moving Guide for Parents. Filled with tons of ideas for parents. If you have children, then this is the book for you and your family. Lori shares insights and advice from her in-depth interviews with parents and from her personal experiences as a mom moving with children. *Moving with Kids* contains lots of great ideas, is well organized, and has twenty-five nice short chapters for quick and easy reading.

Topics include ways to minimize family stress, ideas about how kids can keep old friends and make new ones, how to find the right neighborhood and school, and tips on building children's self-confidence. Comments from kids are also sprinkled throughout.

Corbett, Bill. *Love, Limits, & Lessons: A Parent's Guide to Raising Cooperative Kids.* Enfield, CT: Cooperative Kids Publishing, 2012.

Bill Corbett is an author, a parent education trainer, and founder of the Cooperative Kids organization. His step-by-step approach is based on a firm and respectful discipline that encourages cooperative and responsible children. I enjoyed previewing his videos on his website at www.cooperativekids.com.

Cox, Meg. *The Book of New Family Traditions: How to Create Great Rituals for Holidays & Every Day.* Philadelphia: Running Press Book Publishers, 2003.

I love this book and selected it for my book award for the Creating New Family Traditions category. It's beautifully designed and ideal for parents. If I were a real estate agent, I'd be sure to give this book as a gift to buyers with children who are moving with them.

I have the author's original version published in 2003. Her expanded and updated version, published in 2012, covers twice as many rituals and celebrations. The newer version also spells out tips for using tech tools as you develop your rituals. With Meg's ritual recipes, you can learn how to create rituals from scratch.

Davis, Gabriel. *The Moving Book: A Kid's Survival Guide*. Portland, OR: First Books, 2008.

For children ages 9–12 years old. This book received our top prize for Best Children's Moving Guide. The illustrations by Sue Dennen add much to the enjoyment of this colorful spiral-bound book. The Amazon.com reviews were so favorable, I bought a copy. I love the way it's designed. Very kid-friendly. A supportive resource for children as they face the challenges of moving.

Duncan, Karen, and Kate Hannigan Issa. *The Good Fun Book: 12 Months of Parties That Celebrate Service.* West Bay Shore, NY: Blue Marlin Publications, Ltd., 2010.

For parents with children ages 9–12. Illustrated by Anthony Alex LeTourneau. Not only does Karen and Kate's book dish out lots of great party ideas, but the theme of the fun is to also celebrate a spirit of service to others. Now *that's* fun!

Glasser, Debbie, and Emily Schenck. *New Kid, New Scene: A Guide to Moving and Switching Schools.* Washington, DC: Magination Press, 2012.

For ages 8–13. Debbie Glasser, PhD, and her daughter Emily wrote this book to help new students feel at home in their new school. The guide helps kids discover new ways to express their feelings and face new changes. Chapter topics include being out of one's comfort zone, fitting in, and making friends. Magination Press is published by the American Psychological Association.

Madison, Lynda. *The Feelings Book: The Care & Keeping of Your Emotions.* Middleton, WI: Pleasant Company Publications, 2002.

For ages 8 and up. Illustrated by Norm Bendell. In addition to the American Girl fictional historical books for young girls, the franchise also includes a large selection of nonfiction books covering a variety of topics. This charming and engaging book includes advice for preteen girls on matters of emotions and good ways to face those feelings. Delightful and appealing cartoon illustrations. A companion journal is also available. For a full listing of American Girl resources, visit www.americangirl.com.

Mundy, Michaelene. *Saying Good-Bye, Saying Hello . . . When Your Family Is Moving*. St. Meinrad, IN: One Caring Place/Abbey Press, 2005.

For ages 4–8. Part of the Elf-Help Books for Kids series from One Caring Place. This guide helps young children recognize the fun, joy, fears, and sadness that may come with a move. Charming illustrations by R. W. Alley.

The Teacher's Calendar: The Day-by-Day Almanac of Historic Events, Holidays, Famous Birthdays, and More. School Year 2010–2011 edition. New York: McGraw-Hill, 2010.

For parents and teachers of children kindergarten–grade 8. This great handbook for parents and teachers shares an abundance of interesting events for each calendar day throughout the year. The edition I have (2010–2011 issue) also provides an extensive list of the Newbery and Caldecott Medal book winners and honorees from 1977–2009.

Internet Resources

This Internet Resources section is organized into two groups. The first group covers a variety of general relocation resources to explore. The second group is devoted to websites that assist seniors and caregivers as they plan their moves.

General Internet Resources

Below you'll find a general list of Internet sources you might consider as you plan your move and settle into your new home.

I've included in this list a few do-it-yourself moving resources since a majority of people move locally. When comparing interstate moving companies, be sure the organization is licensed by the Federal Motor Carrier Safety Administration and is assigned a motor carrier number. You can verify that number and also learn ways to prevent moving fraud at www.protectyourmove.gov.

The national organization of movers which adheres to a specific code of ethics is the American Moving & Storage Association at www.moving.org. You can also check with the Better

Business Bureau (www.bbb.org) for individual ratings for different moving companies. And it's always a good idea to seek suggestions and referrals from your real estate agent.

American Automobile Association (AAA)
www.aaa.com

Angie's List (home services listing)
www.angieslist.com

American Moving & Storage Association
www.moving.org

Apartment Guide
www.apartmentguide.com

Apartment Search by CORT
www.apartmentsearch.com

Better Business Bureau
www.bbb.org

Family Support America
www.familysupportamerica.org

Federal Motor Carrier Safety Administration (Department of Transportation)
www.protectyourmove.gov

Google Maps
www.maps.google.com

Home Depot (moving ideas)
www.homedepotmoving.com

HomeFair
www.homefair.com

HomeGain, Your Real Estate Connection
www.homegain.com

International MOMS Club
www.momsclub.org

Just Moved Ministries (Susan Miller)
www.justmoved.org

Mapquest
www.mapquest.com

Move, Inc.
www.move.com

My Moving Reviews
www.mymovingreviews.com

Newcomers Club
www.newcomersclub.com

National Association of Professional Organizers
www.napo.net

National Association of Realtors
www.realtor.com

National Association of the Remodeling Industry
www.nari.org

PODS (moving and self-storage containers)
www.pods.com

Relocation.com LLC
www.relocation.com

Ryder Truck Rental
www.ryder.com

Sperling's Best Places (to live)
www.bestplaces.net

The Heart of Your Move
www.theheartofyourmove.com

U-Haul (moving and storage resource)
www.uhaul.com

Volunteers of America
www.voa.org

Two Men and a Truck
www.twomenandatruck.com

Welcome Wagon
www.welcomewagon.com

Zillow home search
www.zillow.com

Internet Resources for Seniors and Caregivers

American Association of Retired Persons (AARP)
www.aarp.org

American Seniors Housing Association
www.seniorshousing.org

CaringBridge.org
www.caringbridge.org

Creative Potential for Life Transitions (retirement coaching)
www.creativepotential.com

DisabilityInfo.gov
www.disabilityinfo.gov

Elder Cohousing Network
www.eldercohousing.org

Family Caregiver Alliance
www.caregiver.org

Moving for Seniors/Smooth Transitions and Estate Dispersal
www.movingforseniors.com

Moving Station
www.movingstation.com

National Aging in Place Council
www.naipc.org

National Association of Professional Geriatric Care Managers
www.caremanager.org

National Association of Professional Organizers
www.napo.net

National Association of Senior Move Managers
www.nasmm.org

National Association of the Remodeling Industry
www.nari.org

National Council on Aging
www.ncoa.org

National Institute for Aging
www.nia.nih.gov

National Resource Center on Supportive Housing and Home Modification
www.homemods.org

SeniorHousingNet
www.seniorhousingnet.com

Seniors Real Estate Specialists
www.seniorsrealestate.com

Service Corps of Retired Executives (SCORE)
www.score.org

USA.gov for Seniors
www.usa.gov/topics/seniors.shtml

Endnotes

Introduction

1. Anne Morrow Lindbergh, *Gift from the Sea* (New York: Pantheon, 1955).
2. Ibid.
3. William Bridges, *Transitions: Making Sense of Life's Changes* (Reading, MA: Addison-Wesley Publishing Company, Inc., 1980).
4. I've read many books about the human side of change, and William Bridges is my favorite guru in that field. As I mentioned in the introduction, it was a great honor and privilege to learn from the master. He compiled a wealth of information to help guide individuals and companies through the maze of change in a way that respects the human side of the process. Although a number of theories suggest that change is processed in three or four phases, I find Dr. Bridges's approach to make the most sense. He calls his three phases *endings, neutral zone,* and *new beginnings.*

   After my training and certification with Dr. Bridges, he partnered with Linkage, Inc., to provide transition training programs. I felt a great loss when I learned of his recent passing. His wife, Susan Bridges, continues his legacy through the William Bridges and Associates organization. To learn more about his books and transition resources, visit their website at http://wmbridges.com. To learn more about training programs featuring the transition methodology of Dr. Bridges, visit http://www.linkageinc.com.

Chapter 1
Tools to Soften the Stress

1. Mary Anne Radmacher, *Courage Doesn't Always Roar* (San Francisco: Conari Press, 2009). I first discovered Mary Anne's inspirational quote on a self-help website that featured quotations about courage. I later learned that Mary Anne is an artist in addition to being a writer. Her encouraging words and creative images are offered through her books and posters, including the courage quotation at the opening of chapter 1. Mary Ann's website is www.maryanneradmacher.com. Other courage quotations can be found at http://www.self-help-and-self-development.com/courage-quotes.html.
2. Lesléa Newman, *Write from the Heart: Inspiration and Exercises for Women Who Want to Write* (Berkeley, CA: Ten Speed Press, 2003), 13.
3. Julia Cameron, *The Right to Write: An Invitation and Initiation into the Writing Life* (New York: Jeremy P. Tarcher/Putnam, 1998), xvi.
4. YourDictionary, s.v. "courage," accessed May 5, 2011, http://www.yourdictionary.com/courage.
5. Sandra Ford Walston, accessed February 2011, http://www.sandrawalston.com/book/courage/purchase-book. I connected with Sandra through her website and she graciously gave me permission to reprint her citation about courage being your friend. Sandra's website is http://www.sandrawalston.com.

Chapter 2
From Inner Critic to Cheerleader

1. Shakti Gawain, *Creative Visualization* (New York: Bantam, 1978), 30.

2. Abby Seixas, *Finding the Deep River Within: A Woman's Guide to Recovering the Balance and Meaning in Everyday Life* (San Francisco: Jossey-Bass, 2007), 5.
3. Randy Frost et al., "The Dimensions of Perfectionism," *Cognitive Therapy & Research*, 14 (1990): 449-468. Dr. Frost developed a thirty-five-item questionnaire to measure perfectionism called the Multidimensional Perfectionism Scale (MPS). His research also explores levels of parental expectations and criticisms. The Smith College professor is the coauthor of *Stuff: Compulsive Hoarding and the Meaning of Things* (New York: Mariner Books, 2011).
4. Hara Estroff Marano, "Pitfalls of Perfectionism," *Psychology Today*, March 1, 2008, accessed February 14, 2012, http://www.psychologytoday.com/articles/200802/pitfalls-perfectionism. Marano has been the editor-at-large at *Psychology Today* for over fifteen years. She is also the author of *A Nation of Wimps: The High Cost of Invasive Parenting.*
5. Margaret B. Emerson and Catherine Cameron, *Moving: The Challenge of Change* (Nashville: Abingdon Press, 1988.), 67. This is one of my favorite books that honors the heart of moving. Chapters include "The Meaning of a Home" and "Deciding Whether to Move."
6. Free Dictionary, s.v. "affirmation," accessed May 6, 2011, http://www.freedictionary.org/?Query=affirmation. Freedictionary.org aggregates other sources for its definitions. The affirmation definitions cited in this book were from the Wordnet 3.0 source.
7. Mother Teresa, quoted in *Spirit Lifters*, second edition (Lafayette, Colorado: Colorado Church Women United, 1990), April 30.
8. Rosalie Maggio, ed., *An Impulse to Soar: Quotations by Women on Leadership* (New York: Prentice Hall Press, 1998.) 77.
9. Danea Horn, "Affirmation Techniques," accessed May 5, 2011, http://www.creativeaffirmations.com/affirmation-techniques.html.
10. Louise Hay, *Experience Your Good Now! Learning to Use Affirmations* (Carlsbad, CA: Hay House, Inc., 2010), 3.

Chapter 3
Listen to Your Heart Exercises

1. "HeartQuotes: Quotes of the Heart," accessed May 7, 2011, http://heartquotes.net/Heart-quotes.html.
2. http://www.quotationspage.com/quote/3164.html.
3. Audrey McCollum, Nadia Jensen, and Stuart Copans, *Smart Moves: Your Guide through the Emotional Maze of Relocation* (Manchester, NH: Smith and Kraus Publishers, 1996), xii.
4. Susan Jeffers, *Feel the Fear and Do It Anyway* (New York: Ballantine Books/a division of Random House Publishing, 2006), 6.
5. Jennifer Louden, *The Woman's Retreat Book: A Guide to Restoring, Rediscovering, and Reawakening Your True Self—In a Moment, an Hour, a Day, or a Weekend* (San Francisco: HarperCollins Publishers, 1997), 39. Jennifer's books rank at the top of my list of resources that nurture and support a woman's spirit. My husband and I have also much enjoyed her *Couple's Comfort Book* (New York: HarperCollins Publishers, 1994, new edition 2004), which is packed full of great relationship-enhancing information and exercises.

   You can find additional resources at her website, http://www.jenniferlouden.com.
6. Ibid., 41–45 (forming an intention statement for a woman's retreat), 38–47 (intention chapter).
7. Ibid., 41, (creating a positive, compelling, and simple question).

Chapter 4
The Art and Heart of Moving 101

1. Chinese proverb as quoted in William Bridges, *Managing Transitions: Making the Most of Change* (Reading, MA: Addison-Wesley Publishing Company, Inc., 1991), 3. I originally discovered the Chinese proverb in Dr. Bridges's book. The proverb is also listed online at the quotation web page ThinkExist.com, accessed May 8, 2011, http://thinkexist.com/quotation/the_beginning_of_wisdom_is_to_call_things_by/165540.html.

2. Daryl Conner, *Managing at the Speed of Change* (New York: Villard Books, 1995), 155.
3. Martha Poage, *The Moving Survival Guide: All You Need to Know to Make Your Move Go Smoothly* (Guilford, CT: The Globe Pequot Press, 2005), 77.
4. Donna Kozik and Tara Maras, *29 Days to a Smooth Move* (Lincoln, NE: iUniverse, 2005), 109–111.
5. Ariane Benefit (Agile Life Design™ Coach, www.arianebenefit.com) Telephone interview with Barbara McNichol (editor, *The Heart of Your Move*), March 29, 2010.
6. Leslie Levine, *Will This Place Ever Feel Like Home? Simple Advice for Settling In After You Move* (New York: Contemporary Books/a division of McGraw-Hill, 2002), 117.
7. Ibid., 116.

Chapter 5
Create Your Stress Reduction Team

1. Jennifer Sellers, Sheri Boone, and Kate Harper, *Pause: 52 Ways to Shift Any Outcome in Less Than a Minute* (Portland: Inspired Mastery, 2011), 34. I've been blessed with the opportunity to work with Jennifer Sellers, an extraordinary business and life coach. She is one of the founding members of Inspired Learning and Inspired Mastery. For more information about their coaching programs and resources, visit http://www.inspiredmastery.com.
2. Sherie Broekema, ABR, CRS, SRES (Realtor®, Long Realty Company, Tucson, Arizona), telephone interview with Barbara McNichol (editor, *The Heart of Your Move*), March 25, 2010. The comments and suggestions that Sherie shared were accessed from this telephone interview. Sherie's websites are http://www.TucsonHomes.com and http://www.TucsonSeniorResources.com.
3. Kelle Sparta (speaker/author/trainer, Sparta Success Systems). Kelle's website is http://www.spartasuccess.com (real estate agent training).

4. Kelle Sparta, "Help Emotional Clients Keep Their Cool," *REALTOR® Magazine Online*, September 8, 2008, accessed April 28, 2011, http://realtormag.realtor.org/sales-and-marketing/sales-coach/article/2008/09/help-emotional-clients-keep-their-cool.
5. Sharon Harn (consultant, Sharon Harn Organizing), interview via email with the author, December 30, 2010, and January 6, 2011. Sharon's ideas have been integrated into the professional organizer's section of this chapter, which includes benefits, selection, and "5 Tips for De-Stressing Your Move." Sharon is a networking friend from the Tucson Chapter of the National Association of Women Business Owners. I've also been fortunate to receive her consulting advice on several home office projects. Sharon's website is http://www.sharonharn.com.
6. Toni Kane (past president, Newcomers Club of Tucson), telephone interview with Barbara McNichol (editor, *The Heart of Your Move*), March 10, 2010. Toni served a one-year term as president starting June 1, 2009. The website for the Tucson Chapter of the Newcomers Club is http://www.newcomers-cluboftucson.com.
7. Welcome Wagon Social Club of Greater Reading, Berks County, Pennsylvania, accessed April 11, 2011, http://www.welcome-wagonsocialclub.com/. Approval to feature website via email September 22, 2011.
8. Lauren Herring (president and CEO, IMPACT Group, St. Louis, Missouri), telephone interview with Barbara McNichol (editor, *The Heart of Your Move*), March 23, 2010. IMPACT Group's website is http://www.impactgrouphr.com.
9. Ariane Benefit (Agile Life Design™ and productivity coach, http://www.arianebenefit.com), telephone interview with Barbara McNichol (editor, *The Heart of Your Move*), March 29, 2010.
10. I created this story to provide examples of how you can support friends or family members during their health challenges even if you are moving away. The story is dedicated to a special joyful spirit by the name of Valerie Vance Goff, who

cast a warm glow of unconditional love on everyone around her. I'm grateful to Val, to those who encouraged her to create her page on CaringBridge, and for the friends and family who posted their words of care, concern, and love.

CaringBridge.org helps many patients who face health challenges keep in touch with family and friends. This is their mission statement: "As a nonprofit, our mission is to amplify the love, hope, and compassion in the world, making each health journey easier. Our free patient websites bring people together when health matters most." (From www.CaringBridge.org home page, accessed November 10, 2011.)

Chapter 6
Heart-Stages Overview

1. Donna Kozik and Tara Maras, *29 Days to a Smooth Move* (Lincoln, NE: iUniverse, 2005), 130.

Chapter 7
Gracious Goodbyes Heart-Stage

1. Henry Wadsworth Longfellow, "Elegiac Verse," *In the Harbor,* 1879, st. 14, line 1. Although I've seen this quotation frequently in my studies about the nature of change, I discovered a different focus when I read the entire poem. Longfellow's poem features his thoughts about poetry and writing. The quotation is available at numerous online sources featuring Longfellow's poetry, including http://en.wikisource.org/wiki/Elegiac_Verse, accessed October 24, 2011.
2. The definitions for *gracious, goodbye,* and *endings* are composites from multiple sources, including my personal definitions of these words. The sites www.yourdictionary.com and www.freedictionary.org also provided inspiration for the definitions.
3. Angela Smith (owner, Accu-Assist.com) contributed tips via email. Permission to print list, May 12, 2011.
4. An adaptation of the definition from http:// www.yourdictionary.com (LoveToKnow Corp, 1996–2011), s.v. "connection,"

accessed October 24, 2011, http://www.yourdictionary.com/connection.

5. Carol Gray is the author of *The New Social Story Book* (Arlington, Texas: Future Horizons, Inc., 2000) and director of the Gray Center, a nonprofit organization. According to the center's website, Social Stories affirm what an individual is doing well and help improve understanding of events. Further information and video lessons about Social Stories can be found at the center's website at http://www.thegraycenter.org. The expressions "social story" and "social stories" are trademarks owned by Carol Gray.
6. For this account, I used an essay written by my sister, Mary Freeland, that highlighted the ideas she implemented to help her daughter's transition away from home to supported living. Mary also created a social story for Sara that featured her and her husband's move to Lafayette, Indiana. Original essay emailed to author on April 15, 2011. Final narrative approved by Mary on February 7, 2012.
7. Ciji Ware, *Rightsizing Your Life: Simplifying Your Surroundings While Keeping What Matters Most* (New York: Springboard Press/a division of Hachette Book Group USA, 2007), 137.
8. Karen Kovacs (director of sales, Splendido at Rancho Vistoso), telephone interview with Barbara McNichol (editor, *The Heart of Your Move*), March 20, 2010. Splendido website is at http://www.splendidotucson.com.
9. Betty's story and downsizing tips were crafted from multiple conversations with the author over a decade ago. Betty's actual name was changed and several related details were added to this example.
10. Judith Viorst, *Necessary Losses: The Loves, Illusions, Dependencies, and Impossible Expectations That All of Us Have to Give Up in Order to Grow* (New York: Fawcett Gold Medal, 1986), 3.
11. Additional photo books and photo gift ideas can be found at Picaboo.com (Picaboo Corporation), http://www.picaboo.com/ and Shutterfly.com (Shutterfly, Inc.), http://www.shutterfly.com/photo-gifts. For those of you who take photos with your

iPhone, Apple offers similar services, which they describe at http://www.apple.com/ilife/print-products.html.

12. Many of you are knowledgeable and savvy with today's social networking options. Skype is a special visual way of keeping connected. Skype provides free downloadable software that allows you to make video calls on the computer, mobile phone, and television. Using Skype is a great way to keep in touch. My good friend Ann uses it to communicate with her children who live in other states and overseas. I've also seen many examples of military personnel keeping in touch with their families via Skype. Check out http://www.skype.com for details about their services and equipment requirements.
13. Natalie's story and tips in "When the Shoe is on the Other Foot" were inspired by a conversation with the author. The names and details were changed for this example.
14. Angela's tip from "When the Shoe is on the Other Foot" was submitted via email by Angela Smith, owner, Accu-Assist.com. Approval to print, May 17, 2011.
15. Rachel Ballon, *The Writer's Portable Therapist: 25 Sessions to a Creative Cure* (Avon, MA: Adams Media, 2007), 97.

Chapter 8
Muddled Middle Heart-Stage

1. ThinkExist, accessed October 25, 2011, http://thinkexist.com/quotes/marilyn_ferguson/.
2. Marsha Sinetar, *Do What You Love, The Money Will Follow: Discovering Your Right Livelihood* (New York: Dell Publishing, 1987), 1.
3. William Bridges, *Managing Transitions: Making the Most of Change* (Reading, MA: Addison-Wesley Publishing Company, Inc., 1991), 37.
4. The definitions for *muddled/confused* are composites from multiple sources, including my personal definitions for these words. Yourdictionary.com and freedictionary.org also provided inspiration for the definitions.

5. Daryl Conner, *Managing at the Speed of Change: How Resilient Managers Succeed and Prosper Where Others Fail* (New York: Villard Books, 1995), 28.
6. Hope Edelman, *Motherless Daughters: The Legacy of Loss* (Reading, MA: Addison-Wesley Publishing Company, 1994), xx.
7. Leslie Levine, *Will This Place Ever Feel Like Home? Simple Advice for Settling In After You Move* (New York: Contemporary Books/a division of McGraw-Hill Companies, 2002), 13.
8. Meg Files (author/English and Journalism Department chair, West Campus, Pima Community College, Tucson, Arizona), telephone interview with Barbara McNichol (editor, *The Heart of Your Move*), April 1, 2010. Meg also inaugurated and continues to coordinate the annual Pima Writers' Workshop on campus each year (which is held on the weekend of Memorial Day), as well as other creative writing workshops throughout the year. Her website is http://www.megfiles.com.
9. Angela Smith, my virtual assistant, was helping me with a project when I learned that her mother's home in Joplin, Missouri, sustained damage during the 2011 tornado. One of Angela's subsequent trips to Joplin from her home in Oklahoma was to help her mother save some of the flowers and shrubs her late father had planted and nurtured when she was a child. I was deeply moved by her story. I'm grateful to Angela for allowing us to publish this story. Final text approved by Angela on April 29, 2012, via email. Her website is http://www.accu-assist.com.
10. Sundaze Yogurt, 4777 E. Sunrise Drive, Suite 139, is located at the northeast corner of N. Swan Road and E. Sunrise Drive in the foothills area of Tucson, Arizona. My favorite frozen yogurt flavors are banana cream pie and red velvet cake. Yummy.
11. Julia Cameron, *The Artist's Way: A Spiritual Path to Higher Creativity* (New York: Jeremy P. Tarcher/Perigee, 1992), 83.
12. AnnaLisa Michalski, Sunny Words Writing Services, assisted me in collecting the military examples and stories featured in the book. Information was gathered via email interviews and stories were finalized March 20, 2013. The names in the

examples have been changed. AnnaLisa's website is http://www.sunnywords.com.

13. The ideas for "Social Media Tips for You and Your New Job" were excerpted from an article that Alexa, my personal assistant, wrote for me during the time the book was written. Her complete article titled "Technology that Keeps Us Connected" was dated April 17, 2013 and will be posted in its entirely on *The Heart of Your Move* website after this book's publication.
14. Lesléa Newman, *Write from the Heart: Inspiration and Exercises for Women Who Want to Write* (Berkeley: Ten Speed Press, 2003), 6.

Chapter 9
Harmonious Hellos Heart-Stage

1. Sara Ban Breathnach, *Simple Abundance: A Daybook of Comfort and Joy* (New York: Warner Books, 1995), June 8 essay, "In Praise of Real-Life Dining Rooms."
2. The definitions for *hello/welcome, harmonious,* and *home* are composites from multiple sources, including my personal definitions of these words. Yourdictionary.com and freedictionary.org also provided inspiration for the definitions.
3. Eva's story is inspired by ideas from volunteers and the uplifting article in *USA WEEKEND Magazine* (September 24–26, 2010 issue, page 16). Make A Difference Day, the largest national day of helping others, is a *USA TODAY* initiative, backed by the Gannett Company and TEGNA Inc. in partnership with Points of Light and Newman's Own. Make A Difference Day takes place on the fourth Saturday in October. For additional information about Make A Difference Day, visit http://www.makeadifferenceday.com.
4. Karen Duncan and Kate Hannigan Issa, *The Good Fun! Book: 12 Months of Parties that Celebrate Service* (West Bay Shore, NY: Blue Marlin Publications, 2010).
5. Karen Duncan, "Volunteering Gave Us Time Together," *USA WEEKEND Magazine*, September 24–26, 2010, 16.
6. Earth Day is held each year in April. For more ideas on how

to raise awareness about protecting our planet, check out the movement's website at http://www.earthday.org. The bottom of the home page offers links to a footprint calculator, different campaigns, and ways to take action. At the time of publication, the Billion Acts of Green campaign link was http://www.act.earthday.org.

7. Carole Hyder, *Living Feng Shui: Personal Stories* (Freedom, CA: The Crossing Press, 2001), 12.
8. Terah Kathryn Collins, *The Western Guide to Feng Shui: Room by Room* (Carlsbad, CA: Hay House, Inc., 1999), 161. The author developed and teaches Essential Feng Shui programs through the Western School of Feng Shui based in California. In this book, the expert devotes an entire chapter to "The Home Office—A Powerhouse of Productivity."
9. Here is some additional information about Bob Brier's DVD course. Bob Brier, *The History of Ancient Egypt*, The Great Courses, course 350 (Chantilly, VA: The Teaching Company, 1999), DVD. The Teaching Company, now called The Great Courses, offers a large selection of courses taught by engaging professors. Many programs are available in DVD, CD, and/or downloadable formats. For a listing of their programs, visit http://www.thegreatcourses.com.
10. Alexandra Stoddard, *Living a Beautiful Life: 500 Ways to Add Elegance, Order, Beauty and Joy to Every Day of Your Life* (New York: Avon Books, 1986), 3.
11. Meg Cox, *The Book of New Family Traditions: How to Create Great Rituals for Holidays and Every Day* (Philadelphia: Running Press, 2003), 9.
12. Ibid, "Stuffed Animal Parade," 60.
13. The first information I discovered about Make Up Your Own Holiday Day as listed in the *Chase's Calendar of Events* was online at the colorful website Squidoo.com, http://www.squidoo.com/make-your-own-holiday (accessed May 22, 2011). *Chase's Calendar of Events* is published each year by McGraw-

Hill. It's a pricey reference book, so you might want to see if it's available at your local library. Make Up Your Own Holiday Day information is noted on page 189 of the 2011 edition and cites Thomas and Ruth Roy as the originator and copyright owner of this holiday idea. Wellcat Holidays, accessed May 22, 2011, http://www.wellcat.com/holiday.html.

14. "National Ice Cream Day" information accessed May 22, 2011, http://www.holidayinsights.com/other/icecreamday.htm.
15. Information about chocolate holidays accessed May 22, 2011, http://library.thinkquest.org/2886/foo.htm. This web page offers up lots of fun food holidays. Scroll near the bottom to find the chocolate list.
16. "She's Funny That Way Day," also listed in *Chase's Calendar of Events*, credits Brenda C. Meridith, Dahomey Publishing, for this funny holiday. Brenda is the author of *She's Funny That Way* (Winchendon, MA: Dahomey Publishing, 2003).
17. *The Teacher's Calendar: The Day-by-Day Almanac of Historic Events, Holidays, Famous Birthdays and More*, School Year 2010–2011 edition (New York: McGraw-Hill, 2010).
18. Name a Whole Month ideas are a few of the favorites I selected from the extensive list from McGraw-Hill Professional's website, accessed October 26, 2011, http://www.mhprofessional.com/templates/chases/special-months.php.
19. Eric Anders, "May is National Moving Month," *Moving and Relocation Examiner* online magazine, April 22, 2010, accessed July 8, 2013, http://www.examiner.com/moving-and-relocation-in-national/may-is-national-moving-month.
20. Lori Collins Burgan, *Moving with Kids: 25 Ways to Ease Your Family's Transition to a New Home* (Boston: The Harvard Common Press, 2007), 75.
21. Rachel Bertsche, *MWF Seeking BFF: My Yearlong Search for a New Best Friend* (New York: Ballantine Books, 2011), 326.
22. Julia Cameron, *The Right to Write: An Invitation and Initiation into the Writing Life* (New York: Jeremy P. Tarcher/Putnam, 1998), xvi.

The Heart of Your Move Personal Journal Pages

1. Victoria Moran, *Younger by the Day: 365 Ways to Rejuvenate Your Body and Revitalize Your Spirit* (San Francisco: HarperSanFrancisco, 2004), 9.
2. Christina Baldwin, *Life's Companion: Journal Writing as a Spiritual Practice* (New York: Bantam Dell, 1990), 3.

Bibliography

Books, Articles, Quotation References, and Online Journals

Anders, Eric. "May is National Moving Month." *Moving and Relocation Examiner* online magazine, April 22, 2010. Accessed July 8, 2013. http://www.examiner.com/moving-and-relocation-in-national/may-is-national-moving-month.

Baldwin, Christina. *Life's Companion: Journal Writing as a Spiritual Practice.* New York: Bantam Dell, 1990.

Ballon, Rachel. *The Writer's Portable Therapist: 25 Sessions to a Creative Cure.* Avon, MA: Adams Media, 2007.

Bertsche, Rachel. *MWF Seeking BFF: My Yearlong Search for a New Best Friend.* New York: Ballantine Books, 2011.

Breathnach, Sara Ban. *Simple Abundance: A Daybook of Comfort and Joy.* New York: Warner Books, 1995.

Bridges, William. *Transitions: Making Sense of Life's Changes.* Reading, MA: Addison-Wesley Publishing Company, Inc., 1980.

———. *Managing Transitions: Making the Most of Change.* Reading, MA: Addison-Wesley Publishing Company, Inc., 1991.

Burgan, Lori Collins. *Moving with Kids: 25 Ways to Ease Your Family's Transition to a New Home*. Boston: The Harvard Common Press, 2007.

Cameron, Julia. *The Artist's Way: A Spiritual Path to Higher Creativity*. New York: Jeremy P. Tarcher/Perigee, 1992.

——. *The Right to Write: An Invitation and Initiation into the Writing Life*. New York: Jeremy P. Tarcher/Putnam, 1998.

Chinese proverb. ThinkExist.com. Accessed May 8, 2011. http://thinkexist.com/quotation/the_beginning_of_wisdom_is_to_call_things_by/165540.html.

Collins, Terah Kathryn. *The Western Guide to Feng Shui: Room by Room*. Carlsbad, CA: Hay House, Inc., 1999.

Conner, Daryl. *Managing at the Speed of Change: How Resilient Managers Succeed and Prosper Where Others Fail*. New York: Villard Books, 1995.

Copans, Stuart, Nadia Jensen, and Audrey McCollum. *Smart Moves: Your Guide through the Emotional Maze of Relocation*. Manchester, NH: Smith and Kraus Publishers, 1996.

Cox, Meg. *The Book of New Family Traditions: How to Create Great Rituals for Holidays and Every Day*. Philadelphia: Running Press, 2003.

Duncan, Karen. "Volunteering Gave Us Time Together." *USA WEEKEND*, September 24–26, 2010.

Duncan, Karen, and Kate Hannigan Issa. *The Good Fun! Book: 12 Months of Parties that Celebrate Service*. West Bay Shore, NY: Blue Marlin Publications, 2010.

Edelman, Hope. *Motherless Daughters: The Legacy of Loss*. Reading, MA: Addison-Wesley Publishing Company, Inc., 1994.

Emerson, Margaret B., and Catherine Cameron. *Moving: The Challenge of Change*. Nashville: Abingdon Press, 1988.

Ferguson, Marilyn. ThinkExist.com. Accessed October 25, 2011. http://thinkexist.com/quotes/marilyn_ferguson/.

Frost, Randy et. al. "The Dimensions of Perfection." *Cognitive Therapy & Research* 14 (1990): 449–468.

Gawain, Shakti. *Creative Visualization*. New York: Bantam, 1978.

Hamilton, Roberta Sage. *HeartQuotes: Quotes of the Heart*. Accessed May 7, 2011. http://heartquotes.net/Heart-quotes.html.

Hay, Louise. *Experience Your Good Now! Learning to Use Affirmations*. Carlsbad, California: Hay House, Inc., 2010.

Horn, Danea. "Affirmation Techniques." Accessed May 5, 2011. http://www.creativeaffirmations.com/affirmation-techniques.html.

Hyder, Carole. *Living Feng Shui: Personal Stories*. Freedom, CA: The Crossing Press, 2001.

Jeffers, Susan. *Feel the Fear and Do It Anyway*. New York: Ballantine Books/a division of Random House Publishing, 2006.

Kozik, Donna, and Tara Maras. *29 Days to a Smooth Move*. Lincoln, NE: iUniverse, 2005.

Levine, Leslie. *Will This Place Ever Feel Like Home? Simple Advice for Settling In After You Move*. New York: Contemporary Books/a division of McGraw-Hill, 2002.

Lindbergh, Anne Morrow. *Gift from the Sea*. New York: Pantheon, 1955.

Longfellow, Henry Wadsworth. "Elegiac Verse," *In the Harbor*, 1879, st. 14, line 1. Wikisource.org. Accessed October 24, 2011. http://en.wikisource.org/wiki/Elegiac_Verse.

Louden, Jennifer. *The Woman's Retreat Book: A Guide to Restoring, Rediscovering, and Reawakening Your True Self—In a Moment, an Hour, a Day, or a Weekend*. San Francisco: HarperCollins Publishers, 1997.

Maggio, Rosalie, ed. *An Impulse to Soar: Quotations by Women on Leadership.* New York: Prentice Hall Press, 1998.

Marano, Hara Estroff. "Pitfalls of Perfectionism." *Psychology Today,* March 1, 2008. Accessed February 14, 2012. http://www.psychologytoday.com/articles/200802/pitfalls-perfectionism.

McCollum, Audrey, Nadia Jensen, and Stuart Copans. *Smart Moves: Your Guide through the Emotional Maze of Relocation*. Manchester, New Hampshire: Smith and Kraus Publishers, 1996.

Meridith, Brenda C. *She's Funny That Way*. Winchendon, MA: Dahomey Publishing, 2003.

Moran, Victoria. *Younger by the Day: 365 Ways to Rejuvenate Your Body and Revitalize Your Spirit.* San Francisco: HarperSanFrancisco, 2004.

Newman, Lesléa. *Write from the Heart: Inspiration and Exercises for Women Who Want to Write*. Berkeley: Ten Speed Press, 2003.

Poage, Martha. *The Moving Survival Guide: All You Need to Know to Make Your Move Go Smoothly*. Guilford, CT: The Globe Pequot Press, 2005.

Radmacher, Mary Anne. *Courage Doesn't Always Roar*. San Francisco: Conari Press, 2009.

Roy, Thomas and Ruth. "Make Up Your Own Holiday." Wellcat Holidays. Accessed July 31, 2013. http://www.wellcat.com/spring.htm. (Also listed in *Chase Calendar of Events*, 2011 version, 198.)

Seixas, Abby. *Finding the Deep River Within: A Woman's Guide to Recovering the Balance and Meaning in Everyday Life*. San Francisco: Jossey-Bass, 2007.

Sellers, Jennifer, Sheri Boone, and Kate Harper. *Pause: 52 Ways to Shift Any Outcome in Less Than a Minute*. Portland: Inspired Mastery, 2011.

Sinetar, Marsha. *Do What You Love, The Money Will Follow: Discovering Your Right Livelihood*. New York: Dell Publishing, 1987.

Sparta, Kelle. "Help Emotional Clients Keep Their Cool." *REALTOR® Magazine Online*, September 8, 2008. Accessed April 28, 2011. http://realtormag.realtor.org/sales-and-marketing/sales-coach/article/2008/09/help-emotional-clients-keep-their-cool.

Stoddard, Alexandra. *Living a Beautiful Life: 500 Ways to Add Elegance, Order, Beauty, and Joy to Every Day of Your Life*. New York: Avon Books, 1986.

Teresa, Mother. *Spirit Lifters*, second edition. Lafayette, Colorado: Colorado Church Women United, 1990.

The Teacher's Calendar: The Day-by-Day Almanac of Historic Events, Holidays, Famous Birthdays and More. School Year 2010–2011 edition. New York: McGraw-Hill, 2010.

Viorst, Judith. *Necessary Losses: The Loves, Illusions, Dependencies, and Impossible Expectations That All of Us Have to Give Up in Order to Grow*. New York: Fawcett Gold Medal, 1986.

vos Savant, Marilyn. *The Quotation Page*. Accessed June 20, 2013. http://www.quotationspage.com/quote/3164.html.

Walston, Sandra Ford. *Courage*. Accessed February, 2011. http://www.sandrawalston.com/book/courage/purchase-book.

Ware, Ciji. *Rightsizing Your Life: Simplifying Your Surroundings While Keeping What Matters Most*. New York: Springboard Press/a division of Hachette Book Group USA, 2007.

Welcome Wagon Social Club of Greater Reading, Berks County, Pennsylvania. Accessed April 11, 2011. http://www.welcomewagonsocialclub.com/.

Index

C

D

P

R

T

About the Author

Carolyn Masters, MS, EdSp, knows firsthand about the ups and downs and the highs and lows of moving. Her own move to Tucson prompted her to study the very nature of change. Since then, Carolyn has spent more than a decade studying and consulting in the area of the human side of change. She is the author of *When Change Is Your Company's Middle Name,* a business handbook of helpful strategies for executives facing change in the workplace.

In addition to earning degrees in educational counseling and administration, Carolyn received training from Dr. William Bridges, one of the country's leading experts in the field of human change. She also completed the executive training program Effecting Change through the Center for Creative Leadership.

In recent years, Carolyn's client type evolved. She found herself connecting with more and more women much like she had been: those experiencing the challenge of pulling up their roots and moving to a new location.

She was inspired by her clients to create *The Heart of Your Move,* a special handbook designed to encourage women who are facing the stress of moving. Her goal was to provide a wide collection of heartfelt stories and strategies to boost a woman's spirit during her relocation.

Carolyn lives in sunny Tucson, Arizona, with her husband and their adorable dachshund. Her passions include writing, reading British mysteries, relaxing with family, and enjoying gorgeous views of the Catalina Mountains.

To learn more about the author and *The Heart of Your Move,* visit her website at www.theheartofyourmove.com.

The Heart of Your Move

Personal Journal Pages

Often when you start to write your worries,
you find yourself writing their antidote.

—Victoria Moran, *Younger by the Day*[1]

With the craziness of moving, it's important to carve out some private time to explore what your heart is telling you. Christina Baldwin writes in her book *Life's Companion* about the urge to write down your journey, to bear witness to your experience, and to share your questions and insights that come from questioning.[2]

What are your heart-of-moving questions? What part of your relocation journey needs a stress-buster? How can you fill your spirit with words that reflect self-care and encouragement?

Use these pages to jot down your ideas, feelings, thoughts, and reflections anytime as you read through this book and afterwards.

♥ The Heart of Your Move ♥

Personal Journal Pages

♥ The Heart of Your Move ♥

Personal Journal Pages

♥ The Heart of Your Move ♥

Personal Journal Pages

♥ The Heart of Your Move ♥

Personal Journal Pages

♥ The Heart of Your Move ♥

Personal Journal Pages

♥ The Heart of Your Move ♥

Personal Journal Pages

CPSIA information can be obtained at www.ICGtesting.com
Printed in the USA
BVOW08s0637300316

442282BV00002B/196/P

9 781604 949254